THE BOOK OF
BUDLEIGH SALTERTON

From Salt to Watering-Place

D. RICHARD CANN

HALSGROVE

First published in Great Britain in 2005

Frontispiece photograph: *The High Street, 1930s.* (STEVE RICHARDSON)

British Library Cataloguing-in-Publication Data.
A CIP record for this title is available from the British Library.

ISBN 1 84114 406 1

HALSGROVE

Halsgrove House
Lower Moor Way
Tiverton, Devon EX16 6SS
Tel: 01884 243242
Fax: 01884 243325
E-mail: sales@halsgrove.com
Website: www.halsgrove.com

Printed and bound in Great Britain by CPI Bath

*Whilst every care has been taken to ensure the accuracy of the
information contained in this book, the publisher disclaims responsibility
for any mistakes which may have been inadvertently included.*

FOREWORD

On speaking to both townsfolk and visitors one hears many different descriptions of Budleigh Salterton: some call it God's waiting-room, others describe it as sleepy or say that it is caught in a time warp. All agree, however, that Budleigh Salterton is a unique and beautiful place.

Over the years Budleigh Salterton has changed dramatically and in some eyes not necessarily for the better. Many dwellings in the main street were turned into shops, whilst others were lost completely. A severe blow to the town was the loss of the railway station and its aftermath: the sad demise of the large hotels. In 2004, flats occupy the sites where the hotels once prospered.

Despite being a small town with a population of around 5,000, Budleigh Salterton provides much in the way of entertainment and leisure activites, to the surprise and delight of both new residents and visitors. You can kick a ball about or hit one, as is your want, whilst enjoying a game of football, cricket, golf or tennis. Croquet, fishing, bowls and bridge are also popular with the more sedate amongst us. Other available activities include darts, skittles, euchre, bingo, line-dancing, horse-riding and shooting.

In cooperation with the residents of Budleigh Salterton, both the Town Council and the Otter Valley Association are striving to ensure that any changes made to the town have a positive impact. We want to ensure that all future visitors also go home describing Budleigh Salterton as a unique and beautiful place.

If you are a local, I hope that reading this excellent book will remind you of things you haven't thought about in years. If you have only recently come to make your home in Budleigh Salterton, this book will surely enable you to understand why, in this place, time often seems to have stood still. Finally, if you are a visitor to our town, in the words of the motto on the town crest, I wish you 'Beau Sejour', i.e. 'have a beautiful stay'.

Alan L. Jones
Town Mayor
Budleigh Salterton
July 2004

Views of Budleigh Salterton, c.1900.　　　　　　　　(STEVE RICHARDSON)

The catch, 1900s.　　　　　　　　(STEVE RICHARDSON)

CONTENTS

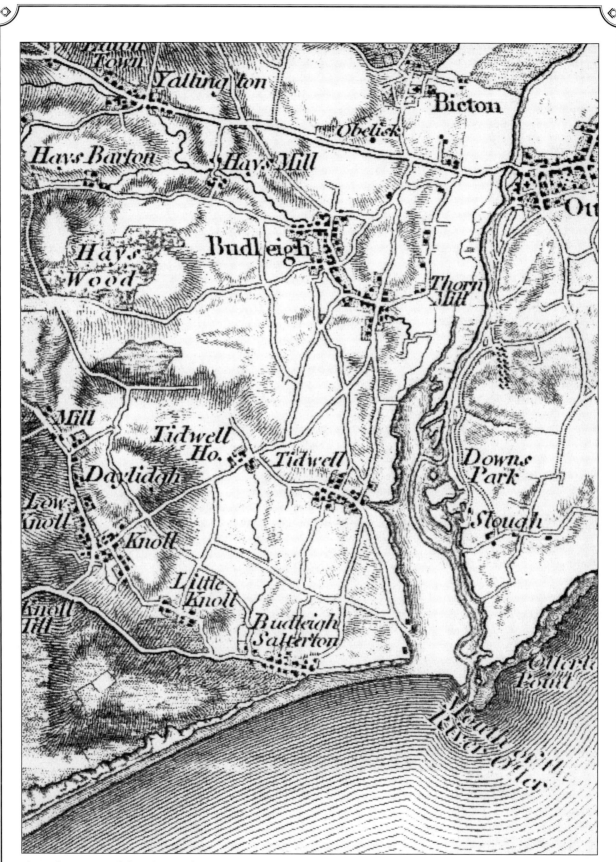

An enlargement of the 1809 Ordnance Survey map (scale: 1in to 1 mile). Note the size of Budleigh Salterton compared to East Budleigh (then known simply as Budleigh). (WESTCOUNTRY STUDIES LIBRARY)

Acknowledgements

The fascinating selection of photographs in this volume represents a community effort. Many people supplied treasured pictures in order that they might be preserved in published form. Their postcards and photographs have succeeded in breathing life back into the events and people in Budleigh Salterton's past.

I am as grateful to those people who supplied a couple of items as I am to those who gave me access to their vast collections. Many thanks to the following: Tom Oates, Julia Meredith, Wendy Morrish, Phillip Leat, Peter McMillan, Revd David Haxell of the Baptist Church, Revd Robert Charles of St Peter's Church, Revd Philip Morse of the Temple Methodist Church, Frieda Lovesy of the Temple Methodist Church for assisting me with their photo archive (as well as those who contributed to that archive) and also Revd Janice Cackett for allowing me to take photographs within All Saints' Church, East Budleigh.

I am extremely grateful to Steve Richardson for allowing me to retain his valuable collection of postcards in order to select those I thought appropriate for this work. Thanks also to Nick Loman for spending time with me whilst selecting pictures from his collection and to those who contributed pictures towards his collection.

I would especially like to thank Kath Gooding, a remarkable lady in her mid-90s with an alert mind and a good memory. Prior to the first occasion that I visited Kath to look at photographs in her possession, I had never met her, but she was about to bring our two worlds closer together. On looking at a picture of a football team within the pages of my first Halsgrove publication *The Book of Bridestowe*, she pointed to one of the players and exclaimed, 'That's my uncle!'. We had a lot to talk about before eventually turning to my purpose for visiting her, Budleigh Salterton.

Thanks are also due to the staff of the Exmouth Reference Library, the Devon Record Office, the Westcountry Studies Library and Ian Maxted of the Devon Library Services. I am grateful to John Varley for giving me permission to use Clinton Devon Estate archive material and to Gerald Millington for showing me around the archive. Thanks also to Richard Tarr of Exmouth for giving me permission to use photos taken by him; these are mainly to be found in Chapters 7 and 10.

I am indebted to Tony Lake for allowing me to use his thesis on the Budleigh Salterton schools. For this I am most grateful.

I also thank Alan Jones, Mayor of Budleigh Salterton for writing the foreword to this book and George Lisle for taking the time to read through the manuscript. Finally, I thank my wife for suffering yet again my history, history, history…

D. Richard Cann
Exmouth
July 2004

Budleigh Salterton

Beautiful place by the wide spreading ocean,
Up to its base does the salt water flow;
Dashing its waves, that are ever in motion,
Lightly upon the smooth pebbles below.
Ever its pure air is sought by the stranger,
Invalids seek not in vain to find health;
Glad to return there is many a ranger,
Home to their birthplace, their prize above wealth.

Scenery! Oh where is there any excel it?
Along by the cliff where such range for the eye!
Little the power in my pen lies to tell it,
Tis but a failure by others who try.
Even the wanderer will seek his own nation,
Rich with the spoils foreign lands to him cast;
Thrill does his heart as the ship nears its station,
Old England and home, he will seek thee at last!
Never more (I should think) would that truant son roam,
If perchance this acrostic above spells his home.

T. Andrews
Photographer
High Street
Budleigh Salterton, 1900.

INTRODUCTION

Budleigh Salterton evolved from a place where salt was produced to a small fishing village. During the seventeenth and eighteenth centuries, owing to the 'salubrious air' that was thought beneficial for 'invalids', i.e. people of a sickly nature, the fishing village developed into the watering-place of Budleigh Salterton. Outgrowing East Budleigh, Budleigh Salterton became a parish in its own right towards the end of the nineteenth century.

At the height of its popularity Budleigh Salterton abounded with hotels and lodging-houses but when the day-tripper replaced the holiday-maker they fell into decline. What can be said in favour of Budleigh Salterton though, is that over the years it has never succumbed to gaudy commercial attractions – the fate of many other seaside towns.

Whilst researching this account of Budleigh Salterton I mostly restricted my sources to those available at the Westcountry Studies Library and the Devon Record Office in Exeter rather than using local facilities. My intention for doing this was to avoid repetition of material already in print.

Within these pages you will not find an account of whose house or shop stood where. Those in search of such information should consult Maria Gibbons's *Budleigh Salterton in the Last Jubilee* and Richard Woodall's *Budleigh Salterton – as it used to be*. The former, written at the time of Queen Victoria's diamond jubilee and looking back through history as far as the diamond jubilee of King George III, and the latter, written in 1954, are of course, in need of an update.

Doubtless some readers will feel that certain aspects of parish life are missing. I apologise in advance for any omissions as I do for any inadvertent errors that may have crept in, particularly with regards to the dates of pictures and the names of the people in them. I hope, however, that this book will help readers to visualize how our predecessors lived, and enable them to form their own conclusions about parish life in bygone days.

Finally, I hope that this account inspires someone else to embark upon a much more detailed history of Budleigh Salterton than these pages allow.

Budleigh Salterton fishermen, late 1800s. (NICK LOMAN COLLECTION)

A colourful postcard for Budleigh Salterton.
(NICK LOMAN COLLECTION)

Chapter 1

From Salt to Watering-Place

Both invalids and Anglo-Indians once aspired to take up residency at Budleigh Salterton. Its position on the east coast of Devon was said to be beneficial to the health conditions of the former, whilst the latter merely enjoyed the climate. Today, Budleigh Salterton's pleasant climate may be viewed as being just as conducive to the health of invalids as it was 100 or more years ago.

Lying south-east of Exeter, approximately 11 miles (as the crow flies) from the county capital of Devon, Budleigh Salterton became a parish in the last decade of the nineteenth century, relatively late when compared with other Devonshire parishes. We are reminded of this fact in an anonymous article published in the *Express and Echo* during May 1937. Budleigh Salterton, so we are told, was 'not able to boast of that antiquity which makes so many Devonshire towns and villages such happy hunting grounds for the antiquarian'.

Nevertheless, the writer goes on to describe Budleigh Salterton as having:

a compensating charm in the loveliness which is so pleasing to the eye, and in that quietude so soothing to tired nerves. In these days when noise has all but swept the entire land like a tidal wave, such places as Budleigh Salterton are like the green oases which dot the desert. Here the tired traveller may rest awhile in the sure knowledge that body and mind will be refreshed.

Whilst criticising other small seaside towns for sacrificing their individuality by trying to become 'a sort of Blackpool in miniature', the author praises Budleigh Salterton for retaining:

that restfulness which belonged to it over a century ago when, in contrast with its spick and span smartness of to-day, it was only an unpretentious fishing village.

Budleigh Salterton Promenade from the east, 1900s. (STEVE RICHARDSON)

Budleigh Salterton was, however, more than just a fishing village. During the eighteenth century it had developed into a watering-place, this being a time when many coastal resorts emerged.

A Brief History

Prior to its separation from East Budleigh by the Local Government Act of 1894, Budleigh Salterton had evolved from a small place, located within the manor of East Budleigh, known as Salterton. The assertion that Budleigh Salterton cannot 'boast of antiquity' is therefore quite untrue. As we shall see, the fascinating history of Salterton offers an insight into the origins of the 'watering-place' Budleigh Salterton.

During the eleventh century, East Budleigh was simply 'Budleigh' and lay in the Hundred of Budleigh, this being a division for county administrative purposes. At this time the Hundred of Budleigh was unusual in that it also consisted of one separate group of parishes situated to the north of Tiverton, and another to the east of Crediton.

The latter part of the eleventh century saw England being surveyed by King William and in the resulting Domesday Book of 1086, East Budleigh is found as 'Bodelie'. In 1333 the detached portions of the Hundred of Budleigh were known as 'West Budleigh', whilst the main portion of the Hundred of Budleigh was 'Estbudlegh' in 1383 and 'Estbodelegh' in 1412. It is from this time that Budleigh acquired the prefix 'East'.

The Town of the Salters

Salterton was, quite simply, the town of the 'Salters' who long years ago manufactured salt there by 'process of evaporation'.

Whether the area around Salterton as we know it today was inhabited at the time of Domesday Book cannot be inferred from the entry relating to 'Bodelie'. Whilst villagers, smallholders, pigmen and slaves are recorded, there is, perhaps surprisingly, no mention of fishermen despite the important contribution of fisheries to the local economy. It is possible that a few of the smallholders may have set up their farms in the location unless however, the fear of being subjected to raiders from the sea prevented them from doing so. There is no record of salt-workers or salt-houses. For this we turn to the Otterton entry in Domesday Book where 33 salt-workers are recorded although there is no mention of where they worked. It is possible that the salt-workers of Otterton carried out their own particular method of salt production at the site of what was to become Salterton, then later Budleigh Salterton.

The Origins of Salt Production

Large-scale salt production started in the late-first century AD; it was essential as winter food supplies depended on it. As there was not sufficient sustenance available to feed more than breeding stock during the winter months, the least number of sheep

A view of Budleigh Salterton from the east with bathing machines, 1900s.   (STEVE RICHARDSON)

Budleigh Salterton from the west with passengers embarking on the paddle-steamer, 1900s. (STEVE RICHARDSON)

and cattle required to sustain flocks and herds were kept alive for breeding the following year. Salt, then as now, was important in that it was used for the preservation of the meat obtained from the slaughtered animals; fish was also preserved with salt.

Long before the salt-houses recorded in the Domesday Book, there had been the Anglo-Saxon *salterns* (salt-works) and before that the Roman *salinæ* (salt lakes). The term *salina* also appears in the Domesday Book and embraces all kinds of salt-works from the coastal pans of Devon, to the boilers of Worcester and Cheshire with their salt-houses – this being the most prevalent term used to describe the allied sheds and buildings.

Paying for the Privilege

During the eleventh century salt-workers had to pay for the privilege of producing salt; there were few rent-free salt-pans and rents varied enormously. Payments were made per annum and were mostly in money; occasionally rent was paid by some other means such as salt or fish. The rent paid by Otterton's 33 salt-workers is unfortunately not shown as a separate figure in the Domesday Book entry – it was included in the payment of the whole manor. Details of individual rents are, however, provided by 18 other manors in Devon with either salt-houses or salt-workers. The figures show that

the highest rent was 60d. and the lowest 1d. but on average, 22d. rent was paid per year. Bishopsteignton had 24 salt-houses, the average rent being 5d. for each, whilst Tamerton Foliet, with one salt-house paid 60d. rent. Of Otterton's neighbours, Seaton with 11 salt-houses paid only 11d. rent in total. Beer was said to have four salt-houses which had been 'taken away', that is, not physically removed, but the salt and the profits were enjoyed by owners of another manor. Honiton, with two salt-workers recorded as paying 60d. rent, is too far inland to have its own salt-works so perhaps it was to Honiton that the rent of Beer's salt-houses was given.

Returning to the 33 salt-workers at Otterton, we cannot be sure of how much rent they paid, but the value of Otterton as a whole had risen by 80 per cent from the time of the Norman Conquest to the compilation of the Domesday Book, 20 years later. It is possible that the salt-workers contributed to the increase in Otterton's value – with 30 salt-workers salt production must have been on quite a large scale.

Sites for Salt Manufacture

There are no extant records that give us any indication as to where salt was manufactured along the River Otter. The *Ancient Sites and Monuments Register* is of no help. Brushfield, writing in 1890, states:

Examination of the estuary is almost impossible, owing to the extensive earthworks incident to the enclosure embankment that were carried out in the early part of the present century.

The overseers' accounts of All Saints' Church, East Budleigh, show that a total of 13s. was paid in tax for the salt-works in 1727. It would therefore seem that the salt-works were still in existence within the Budleigh section of the Otter estuary at this time.

A Sacrament Certificate of 1748 gives Matthew Thomas as an 'officer of duties on salt' at East Budleigh. Maps dating from the 1600s give no indications of salt-works around the Otter estuary although Donne's map of 1765 does show the 'Old Saltworks' to the west of the Exe estuary at Powderham.

In an article titled 'The Budleigh Salt Mines' in *Devon and Cornwall Notes and Queries* (vol.33) in 1975, the author J.R. refers to a pamphlet by A.C. Heaviman, dealing with an incident occurring in a salt-mine during the eleventh or twelfth century in which the Prior of Otterton was implicated:

One of his serfs, a local man named Hugo, apparently took down the mine a large quantity of cider to preserve himself from a raging thirst brought on by the salt.

Once down, he pulled down a section of the ladder and either refused to come up again, or was incapable of so doing. This effectively prevented the next shift from coming down and was an early form of 'lock-in'. The Prior, meanwhile, was so enraged that he stood at the top of the shaft shouting imprecations. Hugo finally emerged a day later, doubtless still suffering the effects of his debauch and as no one was about he climbed over the raised side of the shaft and toppled head-first into a barrel of pickled herring which stood awaiting a further load of salt. It was the subsequent coroner's report (an exceptional document, since serfs were usually drowned without any notice taken) that left its mark in the legal records, being the precedent for such a mode of expiry.

The Warren

As previously mentioned, Donne's map shows the site of an 'Old Saltworks' above Powderham, which was often featured in Trewman's *Exeter Flying Post*. In an edition dated March 1779 extensive premises called The Warren 'bordering on the sea coast opposite Exmouth' were advertised for sale, part of which comprised 'a very considerable salt-works of 4 or 5 pans' that could be 'improved by a person who understands that business'.

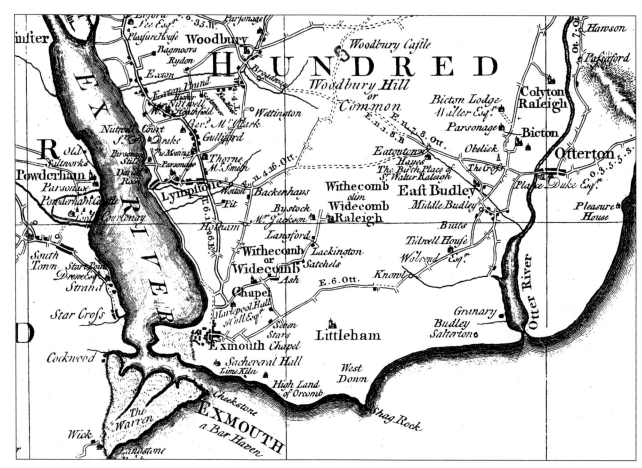

Donne's map of the County of Devon, 1765. Note the 'Old Saltworks' at Powderham. (WESTCOUNTRY STUDIES LIBRARY)

Budleigh Salterton beach from the west, c.1906.   (STEVE RICHARDSON)

Budleigh Salterton Promenade from the west, c.1909.   (STEVE RICHARDSON)

Above: *A view of the Promenade from the west, c.1900.* (NICK LOMAN COLLECTION)

Left: *Passengers landing on the west beach at Budleigh Salterton, 1925.* (KATH GOODING)

The Duchess of Devonshire *beaching at Budleigh Salterton, c.1926.* (STEVE RICHARDSON)

Budleigh Salterton beach from the west, with huts and deck chairs, c.1900. (STEVE RICHARDSON)

March 1784 saw The Warren up for lease to include the 'higher and lower salt-works'. The higher salt-works were all newly built and many tons of salt had been made there the previous summer; the lower salt-works could easily be put into order to make a large and extensive works. Yet again, the December 1789 edition saw The Warren 'including a commodious boiling house' and works for the manufacture of salt, all in good repair, for sale. In the April 1794 edition, we find The Warren up for public auction, the past owners having become bankrupt. The buildings were new but the brine pans, for a small outlay, needed restoring.

From Saltre to Budleigh Salterton

Over 100 years after the compilation of the Domesday Book, the name 'Saltre' appears in a Calendar of Patent Rolls for the year 1210. By 1396, however, the name had changed. In a deed dating from that year, Agnes, the widow of Geoffrey Symeon granted to Warren Bolde a piece of land 'in Salterne'. A further Charter of Agnes dated 1405 mentions 'Salterne in the manor of Buddelegh'.

In November 1438 William Algod granted to Walter Northweche and Agnes, his wife, a piece of land 'in Salterna'. The land granted by William was in exchange for a piece of land in Budleigh called 'Scheytland'.

An Inquisition Post Mortem refers to 'Salteryn' in 1492; Leland writing about the area c.1550 mentions 'Salterton Haven'. During the reign of Elizabeth I, a list of churchwardens for the year 1561–62 gives Richard Hoppen 'of Salterton' but Saxton's map of Devon for 1575 shows the older form of 'Salterne'. In 1600 the East Budleigh churchwardens' accounts record 'malte money' paid by parishioners among which are those from 'Salterton'. A marriage settlement dated 30 May 1653 concerning the wedding of John Willes of Salterton and Susan, his wife, refers to 'Salterton within the parish of East Budleigh'.

'Budley Salterton' appears on Donne's map of Devon dated 1765. As Donne also places Woodbury Salterton on his map it may well be that he uses 'Budley' along with Salterton at this period in order to distinguish the two places. As for the Salterton element of Woodbury Salterton mentioned in an Assize Roll of 1306, it is suggested that the name may well refer to a 'salter's farm', rather than a place where salt was produced, as it is situated well inland.

The numerous maps of the seventeenth and eighteenth centuries are often confusing due to their wide variations in the spelling of place-names; sometimes places are not marked at all. Blome's map of 1673 shows 'Saltern' with a symbol alongside, which appears to indicate a church. However, there was no such edifice in Budleigh Salterton until the nineteenth century. Seale's map of 1732 shows 'Newton' (new town) to the east of the mouth of the Otter, whilst Read's map of 1750 has 'Newton' to the west; Newton Poppleford is also shown so the two are not to be confused. It is likely that by this time the few fisherman's huts at Budleigh Salterton were beginning to multiply, hence 'Newton'.

The direction cross situated where the Otterton road meets the Budleigh Salterton to Newton Poppleton road was erected by Lady Rolle in 1743. Interestingly, one face shows the way 'To Budley, Littleham and Exmouth' but omits Salterton. Perhaps Salterton was not thought of as being of any significance at that time.

An inscription on a floor slab in the south aisle near the rood-loft stairs of East Budleigh church records the death of:

Joseph Comer
of Salterton Gent
Obiit Oct: 14th 1755
Ætat: suæ 67.

In Bowen's map of 1767 the name 'Salcomb' appears instead of 'Salterton'. It would at first seem that Bowen had confused Salterton with Salcombe Regis, but he was not the only one to use this name. Writing in 1799, Robert Southly related the following:

From Ottery I walked with S.T. Coleridge to 'Budley Salcome'... the Otter enters the sea at 'Budley Salcombe.' I forded it at its mouth. The scenery upon the river is tame and soothing; like all the Devonshire rivers it often overflows.

By 1822 Mutlow's map shows 'Budleigh Salterton', as does Walker's map of 1836. From about this time onwards Budleigh Salterton seems to be the accepted name, although a deed regarding mining rights dating from April 1835 mentions 'Saltistown' in East Budleigh.

Brushfield informs us that:

The earliest mention of 'Budleigh Salterton' in the registers is in the year 1813; but it does not occur in the other parish books until a much later date.

An inspection of the headstones in East Budleigh churchyard corroborates this information. There are headstones inscribed with the place-name Budleigh Salterton dating from 1815 and memorial tablets inside the church dating from 1836 onwards.

Birth of the Parish

The civil parish of Budleigh Salterton was created in 1894 upon its separation from the mother parish of East Budleigh. The parish was enlarged on 1 April 1896 when a Local Government Board Order transferred part of the civil parish of Littleham to that of Budleigh Salterton.

On 22 May 1900, an order of council established Budleigh Salterton as a separate ecclesiastical parish. At this time Budleigh Salterton was in the eastern division of the county and formed part of East Budleigh Hundred. In relation to justice it came under Woodbury Petty Sessions and the Exeter County Court District; it was in the St Thomas Union for the administration of the poor, including the workhouse. As for religion, Budleigh Salterton was in the Rural Deanery of Aylesbeare and the Archdeaconry and Diocese of Exeter.

The Boundaries

Budleigh Salterton is bounded on the south by the sea from the mouth of the River Otter in a westward direction for a little over 2 miles to The Floors at West Down Beacon. Along this coastline the cliffs rise in some places from 100 to more than 250ft. From The Floors the boundary follows natural and man-made features along a course back to the mouth of the Otter. Going northwards from The Floors, the boundary traverses a ridge towards Knowle Hill, crossing Littleham church path prior to reaching Heart's Delight, at which point Castle Lane forms the boundary until it meets the old rail track. The boundary then proceeds along the old rail track arcing eastwards passing Leeford, Knowle House and Higher Knowle Farm to Shortwood Lane, which then forms the boundary to its juncture with the B3178, which is then followed as far as Tidwell House. (Initially, the course of the boundary ran from Castle Lane to Knowle Corner, along the road through Knowle Village to Tidwell House.) From Tidwell House the boundary goes to the right, following the lane through Kersbrook, passing Penny Park, Kersbrook Farm and Kersbrook Cottage, before crossing the Budleigh Salterton to East Budleigh Road and the old rail track again. The boundary then turns right to proceed along the footpath on the crest of the embankment that runs nearly parallel to Granary Road until it reaches the south side of the cricket field, at which point it crosses The Saltings to the Otter and then terminates at Otterton Ledge.

According to White's *Directory of Devon* of 1850, Budleigh Salterton covered 977 acres of land, 4 acres of tidal water and 39 acres of foreshore which:

affords incessant occupation and amusement to the

Budleigh Salterton Parish from the 1938 Ordnance Survey map (scale: 6in to 1 mile; reduced).

(CLINTON DEVON ESTATES)

curious and the lovers of natural history in seeking out the moss, agate, jasper, and other rich pebbles and petrifacations, with which it abounds.

The Rise of Budleigh Salterton

The transformation of Leland's sixteenth-century 'Fishar Village… caullid Salterne' to the 'wateringplace' of Budleigh Salterton has been documented by travelling diarists, visitors, and those who made their living through the columns of papers and magazines. These observations offer us an insight into Budleigh Salterton at the time when it was gaining in popularity during the eighteenth and nineteenth centuries. The number of visitors did, however, fall with fashion; the pebbles became less of an attraction and people preferred to spend their precious holiday time on sandy beaches. With the arrival of the railway at the end of the nineteenth century, however, visitor numbers increased once more.

Writing in the late-eighteenth century, Revd Richard Polwhele warns of an impending catastrophe at Salterton in his *History of Devonshire*. Having observed 'considerable defalcations of the

shore', he had no doubt that 'some of the houses at the lower end of the village will be tumbled into the sea, in less than a century'. He also says that:

Salterton, a village on the sea, lies in sight of Torbay. The air of this parish is, in general, wholesome. Of the inhabitants, some occupy farms, leaseholders and rackholders; others are fishermen. Lacemaking is the chief employment of the woman.

A contemporary of Polwhele, the Revd John Swete, was also travelling around Devon at this time. His diary relates that in 1795 after visiting East Budleigh he pursued a track to the little bay formed by a sandbank at the mouth of the Otter, but had problems finding his way to Budleigh Salterton:

leaving by too quick a turn to the left [I] missed the road to the village of Budleigh Salterton which I was in quest of; I had now to pursue my way on a shore of pebbles into which my horse sunk to the knee – to relieve him therefore of part of the pressure I dismounted, and had, as disagreeable a walk of an half mile (for so far had I got to the east of Budleigh) as can be imagined.

19

An empty beach looking towards Otterton Ledge, c.1900.
(STEVE RICHARDSON)

Marine Parade, c.1900.
(STEVE RICHARDSON)

The Promenade looking towards the east, c.1910. (STEVE RICHARDSON)

When he finally reached Budleigh Salterton, Swete was not particularly impressed with what he found:

[I] found little compensation for my toil – the view of the Coast was extensive, but then it was composed of the loosest pebbles, and there was scarce a house that fronted it. The buildings in general of the meanest cast intermingling with trees had a picturesque appearance; but in other respects had so few of those points requisite for a watering-place, that I think its improvement, in equipping a few cottages for Invalids has been carried nearly to its full extent. To many however it possesses, and it is probable will retain, two desiderata of the chiefest import, Retirement, and as genial an air as any on the coast. This last is obvious to the most unobserving eye, in the frequency and luxuriance of the Myrtles – those at Tidwell are indeed superior to any I have seen; and from their requiring no shelter or protection during the inclemencies of Winter, one should almost be led to conclude that the climate was even more mild than that of Italy or at least the part where Virgil resided.

Swete, as Polwhele, gives the occupation of the men as farmers and fishermen and the woman as lacemakers. As for local dishes, he comments on the popularity of lobster as well as a more unusual 'vegetable':

laver – this last under the class of [mosses], is a vegetable growing on the rocks, it is the [ulva] marina or conferva, is an antiscorbutic, and for its flavour is in high request at the tables of many.

Observations from the Early-Nineteenth Century

Haseler, writing just prior to 1818 on the scenery of the South Devon coast, presents an altogether more positive picture of Budleigh Salterton. He thought it:

a very pretty watering-place, and being upon a small scale is more particularly suited to invalids and persons of retired habits, than larger and [gaudy] places.

One year later the interior of All Saints' Church at East Budleigh was enlarged, owing apparently 'to the increasing numbers of parishioners, due to the rise of the village of Budleigh Salterton'. The number of seats was increased by the erection of a gallery measuring the entire length of the north aisle. East Budleigh churchyard was extended 30 years later owing to the number of interments 'much increased by the enlarged and enlarging population of Budleigh Salterton.'

A visitor to the town on 1 September 1820, Miss Wyndham Portman of Salisbury, described it as 'a pretty little bathing place'. This was also the sentiment of Thomas Pougher Russell of Gloucester, who wrote the following in August 1837:

A very nice bathing place – fine view of the sea from several terraces along which were a great number of apparently good lodging-houses as well in other parts of the town which is small but neat, high cliffs near it on which there seems to be fine walks for breathing pure sea air – roads were very bad most of the way along narrow lanes where for considerable distances two carriages could not pass.

Budleigh Salterton during the Mid-Nineteenth Century

On 24 August 1850 an article titled the 'Watering-Places of England' appeared in *The Illustrated London News*. Budleigh Salterton was described as follows:

This charming resort lies about four miles from Exmouth, passing through the sequestered village of Littleham, adown [sic] Knowle Hill. Like many other resorts on the coast, it has risen from a few straggling fishing huts into notice as a watering-place within the present century. It is built along the bottom of a small valley, inclining from north-west to south-east, with buildings rising on each side, the eastern extremity opening towards the sea. The lodging-houses or places of residence for visitors are on the summit and sides of the hills. Through the middle of the main street runs a brook of clear water, across which are two or three wooden bridges: nothing can be more primitive. The beach, which is composed solely of broad, flat, oval-shaped pebble, extends from Otterton point on the east, to the base of Orcombe Hill on the west, a distance of between two and three miles.
The air is light, buoyant, and exhilarating. Rain is not so frequent here as at some other places on the coast. There are hot and cold baths, and bathing machines on the beach. From its pebbly nature, the terrace or marine parade at the south-eastern end of the town, in front of the sea, is the principal promenade. A broad footpath rises from the beach, on the western side, which will take the pedestrian over the cliffs, and to Exmouth.

A more detailed account of Budleigh Salterton in 1850 can be found in White's *Directory of Devon* for that year. The directory could be described as the equivalent of the modern-day *Yellow Pages*, although it also contains a general description of the place concerned, as well as a brief history.

This engraving of Budleigh Salterton is from The Illustrated London News *dated 24 August 1850.*
(WESTCOUNTRY STUDIES LIBRARY)

Population

Up until the year 1901 the population of Budleigh Salterton was included in the figures for East Budleigh. In 1801 the population of the two places was 1,014, rising to 2,319 by 1841. In comparison Exmouth's population rose from 2,601 to 5,119 during this period. These figures show that the population of Exmouth increased by 96.8 per cent, whereas the population of Budleigh Salterton and East Budleigh increased by 128.7 per cent.

By 1871 the combined population of Budleigh Salterton and East Budleigh totalled 2,897. A decrease in population followed, however, with sandy beaches becoming more important than salubrious air; by 1901 the populace had dropped to 2,653.

In 1931 the population of Budleigh Salterton alone was 3,162 rising to 3,865 in 1961 and 4,436 in 1981. At the time of writing the town has a population of about 5,000.

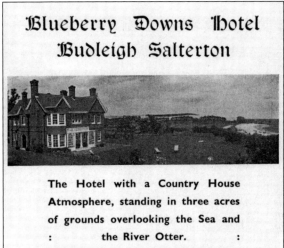

Blueberry Downs Hotel Budleigh Salterton

The Hotel with a Country House Atmosphere, standing in three acres of grounds overlooking the Sea and : the River Otter. :

Clockwise, starting above left: *Hotels at Budleigh Salterton, 1960s: Park House, Blueberry Downs and Nattore Lodge.* (NICK LOMAN COLLECTION)

In 1850 Budleigh Salterton was still listed under East Budleigh. The directory informs us that the East Budleigh parish of 1850, the majority of which was owned by the Trustees of the late Lord Rolle, consisted of 2,620 acres and had a population of 2,319. The parish included the 'pleasant and handsome little town and bathing place of Budleigh Salterton', and the hamlets of Great and Little Knowle which were suburbs of Budleigh Salterton.

The town is described as having one street where the shops and inns were situated, whilst the lodging-houses were located, in the main, on the 'summit and sides of the hills on either side'. The town was within the bounds of the port of Exeter, but had its own Coastguard, consisting of a lieutenant and 11 men. Mackerel and other fish were caught near the bar of the estuary. Swimmers could make use of both hot and cold baths, as well as the bathing machines on the beach. The bookworms of the town were also well catered for: Budleigh Salterton had two circulating libraries and reading-rooms, too. Local children were able to attend the National School, built by Lord Rolle in 1842. A Wesleyan chapel had been erected in 1811 by James Lackington, a London bookseller, at the cost of around £1,700. The church or chapel of ease, Holy Trinity, was built in 1812–13 by Lord Rolle at the cost of £900 and was enlarged in 1837 at the further cost of £1,100. In 1884 a small Baptist chapel was built in Park Terrace, Little Knowle.

Pleasure and pedlary fairs were held at East Budleigh on Easter Tuesday and at Budleigh Salterton on Whit-Tuesday.

A main Post Office was situated in Budleigh Salterton where letters were despatched at 5p.m. and money orders were granted and paid. Coaches departed from the Rolle Arms to Exeter and Sidmouth on a daily basis in the summer and three times a week in winter. Three carriers operated services to Exeter and various other places on Mondays, Tuesdays, Wednesdays and Fridays.

After this summary of the town, prominent parishioners and local tradespeople are listed. Of course telephone numbers were not included at this date, although they appeared in the pages of the much later directories. Listed alongside a number of ladies and gentlemen were the following: eight clergy; two eating-house owners; four lacemakers; one currier; one gardener; two hairdressers; one cider merchant; one lace dealer; one tinner and brazier; one hatter; one basket maker; one bathing machine owner; one stay maker; one gunsmith; two veterinary surgeons; two beer sellers; one lithographer; one lapidary; one cooper; five inns (Feathers, King William IV, Rolle Arms, Queen Victoria and William IV); six fire and life office agents;

four corn millers (Dalditch Mill, Kersbrook Mill, Thorn Mill and Town Mill); seven boarding academies; seven bakers; six blacksmiths; two booksellers; 14 boot- and shoemakers; four butchers; ten carpenters; two coal dealers; 18 farmers; one maltster; six fly (one-horse hackney carriage) owners; ten grocers and drapers; two linen drapers; 20 lodging-house owners; three masons; eight milliners; four painters and plumbers; four shopkeepers; three surgeons; six tailors; two watchmakers and four wheelwrights.

From the directory it is quite clear that Budleigh Salterton was self-sufficient in 1850.

Walter White of London painted a tranquil picture of Budleigh Salterton on his visit in 1855:

This is a village watering-place with a growing reputation, and not undeservedly, for it stands in a valley so narrow and well sheltered that myrtles grow in the open air all the year round and like its namesake in the interior, it has a sprightly brook running by the side of the road crossed by numerous light bridges to the trim gardens in front of the houses. A place of cheerful aspect. From an eminence on the beach the Otter is seen, its vivacity left behind creeping ingloriously through a marshy flat to the sea, where a long reef stretches out at one side of its mouth. The coal merchants here, wiser in their generation than some elsewhere, have laid a tramway across the public shore, along which laden trucks are hauled from the vessel.

[There is] a cliff sided hill on the west... West Down Beacon. Seats are placed at short intervals on the long sloping ascent; and from the top you can get a view of the 3 miles of cliffs you may have missed by the visit to Hayes Barton; and in the other direction, down to Torbay and Berry Head. To an unaccustomed eye there is something surprising in the successive headlands, each stretching farther and farther to seawards that to walk to their extremity seems an endless task, so different from what it appears on the map and you can scarcely help feigning that the last will take you far into the sunny regions of the south. Pacing the coast mile by mile for days together you find England to be not so small a country after all.

Impressions from the Late-Nineteenth Century

Alfred L'Estrange did not share White's sentiments, and wrote c.1872 of Budleigh Salterton that 'the place is so primitive that when there is no starlight the inhabitants go about the dark carrying lanterns'. He also mentioned that before he left Budleigh Salterton 'a quack doctor drove into the town, knocked at all the doors, presented his card, and told the people that they 'looked bilious''.

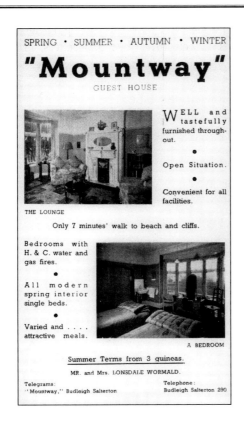

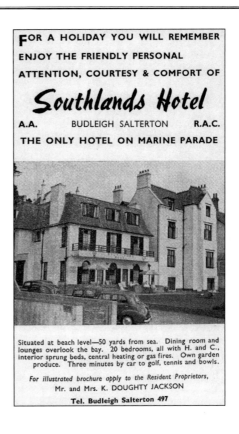

Clockwise, starting above left: *Further hotels, 1960s: Southlands, Mountway and the Long Range which is still functioning in 2004.* (NICK LOMAN COLLECTION)

Amongst the files of newspaper cuttings held in the Westcountry Studies Library is an article titled 'Budleigh Salterton'. There are no clues as to its author, nor to where it was first published. One thing is, however, for sure: two words in this article are not acceptable today, due to their politically incorrect nature. The narrative, with the offensive words omitted and indicated by square brackets, reads in part as follows:

To the busy man, anxious to be free from the whirl and turmoil of town life, and to shake off the effects of unrest and excitement amid calm and peaceful surroundings, Budleigh Salterton is enchanted grounds. The inconvenient conveniences which modern science has provided for saving time and making money have not yet penetrated within its borders. There is no railway, no factory, nothing to suggest commercial activity [...] no mysterious minstrels, no German bands to entice one's thoughts away to boisterous pleasures. Sweet repose reigns supreme. Budleigh nestles between the hills at the mouth of the Otter, just about midway between Exmouth and Sidmouth, and it is in communication with the former town by means of a service of omnibuses, which run to and fro four or five times a day. Another and much pleasanter way for the stranger to reach it is to drive from Exeter, passing over Woodbury Common and through some of the richest scenery in the country. Budleigh is by no means a place in which one need sleep one's time away, although it is a great temptation to lay on the lawns which front the pleasant residences facing the sea in blissful idleness. There is much to be seen, in a quiet way, in the neighbourhood after the morning bathe from the pebbly beach. There are some very pleasant walks over the cliffs by Ladram Bay to Sidmouth, or in a westerly direction to Exmouth. Of the two the latter is perhaps to be preferred, as a much better view of coast scenery is to be obtained, to say nothing of the landscapes, the country inland having all the attractiveness of a carefully laid out park on a very large scale. The drives are exceedingly pretty, Bicton and Woodbury Castle being amongst the places which may be visited. Within an easy distance there are several charming walks; and, to be brief, one can find all that can be wished in the way of healthy exercise without undue exertion. There is every facility for boating and fishing, and the fishing at sea or in the river is of the best. The hotel accommodation is quite sufficient for the place, and apartments in private houses can be secured at moderate rates. The climate at Budleigh is most healthy, being mild, and at the same time bracing. For invalids it is a fine winter resort.

Whilst the author of the above account does not mince his words when alluding to what, in his opinion, would mar Budleigh Salterton, he gives a favourable account of the place. By 'invalids' he simply means people of a sickly nature, and not the modern-day interpretation of the word.

From an article in the *Exeter Gazette* dated September 1897 we learn the following:

the London and South Western Railway has opened up an easy route to the favourite watering-place which will henceforth rejoice in the single name of Salterton, to distinguish it from the pretty but less-popular village of Budleigh, a large number of residents as well as of tourists will most assuredly find their way to this charming resort. Through carriages from both up and down directions offer every inducement to invalids in search of a winter home to make their way to a place where there is the most beautiful air…

We are further informed that 'the necessaries of life are easy obtained': there was an excellent supply of water whilst the drainage and sanitation left 'nothing to be desired'. Salterton was 'blessed with many families of moderate means and refined tastes'. There was at least one first-class school for boys and private tuition was readily available.

The Turn of the Century

In another report, dated July 1902, we are reminded that Millais's portrait of Sir Walter Raleigh as a small boy paying heed to an old tar demonstrated perhaps that 'this sweetly picturesque little town [...] was a worthy and fitting nursery-ground for one of Devon's great sea-dogs.' Further, it was thought that Salterton was a place 'eminently suitable for victims of nervous disorder and brain worry'. The author goes on to describe Budleigh Salterton as:

one of Nature's ideal nooks, and the scene vouchsafed to the incoming visitor as, from the top of the hill, he gains his first peep of the sea and the tall cliffs, and drives down through the quaint main street, half hidden under the trees, and a clear fresh brook jumping merrily alongside, augurs well for the fulfilment of the expectations any enthusiastic admirer of Salterton may have led him to assume. The stream, which, by the way, is said to remain free from pollution in its whole course from the source near the village of Tidwell to the sea, is spanned by rustic bridges leading to pleasant villas, with cheerful gardens, in which the myrtle, the hydrangea, and other plants dear to the English heart flourish vigorously without the aid of artificial protection.

The author goes on to voice a single criticism, not of Budleigh Salterton, but of the people who once lived there:

There is only one reasonable fault to find with Budleigh Salterton, and the blame must be attributed to perverse individuals, probably long ago dead. It would be interesting to know why these people preferred to build a long line of houses at the beginning of the Cliff Walk to West Down Beacon with their backs [i.e. the houses' backs] turned towards the sea, as if they despised the splendid prospect. It is hard for such a beautiful bay to be insulted with back gardens and dismal stone walls. Having indulged in this passing grumble, one can forget the disfigurement and wander up the well-made cliff path right away to the Beacon, 250 feet high, where supposing it to be a fine day, is unfolded a superb panoramic view of sea, coast, and Devonshire hills that once seen can never leave the memory.

As for Budleigh Salterton's famous pebbly beach, the writer reveals how the larger stones had been 'usefully employed in local building operations', whilst the smaller ones appealed to 'young ladies, and, for the matter of that, young men with artistic eye' who took them away 'to grace bureaux or to act as paper-weights or curiosities'.

The town was said to occupy 'an unenviable position in the health records' and had good amenities. The Rolle Hotel in particular was pointed out for 'excellent accommodation', this also being available from other hotels, private apartments and boarding-houses, many of which had 'admirable situations'.

There were many opportunities for relaxation and amusement, such as trout fishing along the banks of the Otter; there was also 'safe and excellent bathing', although 'the banks of pebbles sometimes cause slight inconvenience'. The croquet and tennis club with seven courts was 'extremely popular'; there were also three further croquet grounds and an

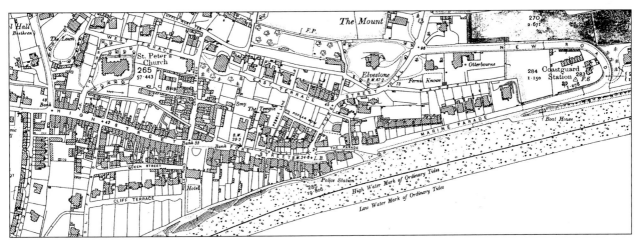

The 1905 Ordnance Survey map (scale: 25in to 1 mile; reduced). The road arcing around the Coastguard Station was known as 'New Road' at this time.

(CLINTON DEVON ESTATES)

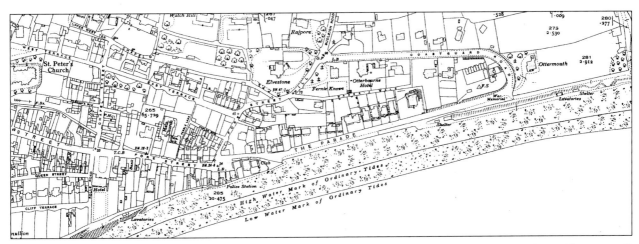

The 1933 Ordnance Survey map (scale: 25in to 1 mile; reduced) now shows 'Coastguard Road' in place of 'New Road' and 'The Mount' of 1905 has now become 'Rajpore', perhaps after having been renamed by an Anglo-Indian.

(CLINTON DEVON ESTATES)

archery field. Mental stimulation was also catered for, in the form of a literary institution, a lending library and a gentlemen's club. A Masonic Hall was the venue for the 'mysterious meeting-place of the 'craft''.

Private dances could be enjoyed by residents and visitors alike, as could sea trips on the *Duke* or *Duchess* steamboats which were said to 'touch – almost literally – the beach in their Channel excursions'. The golf links, which the writer deemed 'worthy to be ranked among the best in the country', had recently opened thanks to the:

enterprise and public spirit of the Hon. Mark Rolle, a lord of the manor who certainly merits the gratitude of the inhabitants by his many acts of generosity and practical sympathy with the proper development of this place.

The writer considers St Peter's Church to be the town's finest building. The Cottage Hospital is described as being 'admirably equipped' and highly beneficial to the inhabitants of the town.

Summing up, our writer says:

Such is Budleigh Salterton at the present day, and, though the rapidity with which it has moved forward of late, thanks to local enterprise, as a town and as a recognised holiday resort rather argues that its day as a place of entire seclusion is passing away, this must be regarded as one of the inevitable results of that modern encroachment which, as the logical outcome of the growth of population, requires as each summer returns an increasing outlet, and renders the eventual publicity of every striking point on the English coast a mere matter of time. It remains to be seen how soon and how materially the effect of the important connecting railway link which is now in course of being constructed from Exmouth to Budleigh Salterton – thus constituting a complete chain of railway from Exeter – will be felt, but in the immense facilities it will afford for the greater accessibility it is bound to operate effectively sooner or later, and the purpose of the line will be unmistakably furthered by the recent establishment of a Golf Club and unrivalled golf links, for, as everybody knows, there are few more potent allurements to a town by the sea than that of links which will give genuine sport to golfers, who are an ever-increasing army, and who are generally too, of the class of visitor who spend money. Without doubt, Budleigh Salterton has a promising future, and has no reason to be afraid of being vulgarised.

The author was obviously convinced that the railway link with Exmouth and Exeter would have an overall positive impact upon Budleigh Salterton. One thing, however, he neglected to foresee: the increasing popularity of sea bathing and sandy beaches. Whereas Exmouth was amongst the first resorts to benefit from this fashion, Budleigh Salterton's pebbly beach no longer appealed to many potential visitors.

At least the new railway link meant that holiday-makers could take a day-trip to Budleigh Salterton. Whether the golf links lured 'the class of visitor who spends money' to Budleigh Salterton is debatable, but the golf links remain in 2004, whilst the railway has gone.

Sickness and Health

The population of Budleigh Salterton enjoyed very good health in the early-twentieth century. The general death rate was 18.3 per 1,000 with more than half the deaths occurring in people over the age of 65. This figure is probably due to the fact that the majority of the residents had moved to Budleigh Salterton in their old age.

As for diseases, contagious infections were rare; blood disorders, pleurisy, acute nephritis (inflammation of the kidneys), rheumatoid arthritis, gout and neuralgia were most uncommon. Acute rheumatism was almost unknown and skin diseases were also rare. The climate benefited those suffering from tuberculous diseases such as bronchitis, asthma, pneumonia, scrofula and phthisis (although the latter seldom originated in Budleigh Salterton). The area was found to be beneficial to those with valvular heart disease, but the country was too hilly for cardiac cases. Sleeplessness was most unusual amongst residents, whilst visitors suffering from this condition improved.

Budleigh Salterton during the Early-Twentieth Century

Writing in 1907, Harper considered Budleigh Salterton to be:

an individual place, without its fellow anywhere. Conceive a brook running in a deep bed down one side of a village street, and bridged at close upon half a hundred intervals with brick and plank footbridges, leading across into cottages and cottage-gardens; and conceive those cottages, partly the humble homes of fishermen, and partly the simple villas of an Early Victorian, or even a Regency, seaside, and midway down the street imagine that stream crossing under the road, taking the little beach diagonally, and there percolating through the giant 'popples'.

The Marine Hotel, Fore Street, c.1906.
(STEVE RICHARDSON)

The Rolle Hotel, mid-1900s.   (STEVE RICHARDSON)

The Rosemullion Hotel, mid-1900s.   (STEVE RICHARDSON)

Below: *A farewell to the Rosemullion Hotel, 1987.* (NICK LOMAN COLLECTION)

BUDLEIGH SALTERTON CHAMBER OF COMMERCE

Dinner & Dance

Farewell to the Rosemullion Hotel

at the Hotel

on Friday 20th NOVEMBER 1987

7.00 pm. for 7.30 pm.

DANCING UNTIL 1.00 am.

TO THE SOUNDS OF 'BITTERSWEET'

Dress D.J.s' or Lounge Suits.   *Tickets £10.00*

Colourful postcards of Budleigh Salterton from the 1920s. (NICK LOMAN COLLECTION)

* ♦ THE FEATHERS ♦ *

The Feathers, 1960s. (STEVE RICHARDSON)

He describes the front of the town as actually being situated:

at the back, for in times before the invention of the seaside as a place of holiday, the inhabitants seem to have had a surfeit of the sea by which they got their living, and built their houses on the low crumbly cliff, not only with the faces turned away from it, but in many cases with high dead walls enclosing back-gardens, entirely excluding any sight of the water. And so the 'front' remains; nor is it clear how, without a wholesale rebuilding, it will ever be otherwise. It is a curious spot, for a seaside resort, and in places more resembles an allotment garden, or the side of one of those railway embankments, where frugal porters and platelayers cultivate vegetables; for between the pathway and the sea, on the fringe of that beach where the gigantic popples lie ranging in size from a soup-plate down to a saucer, and forming the raw material of the local paving, there are rows of potatoes, cabbages, peas, and scarlet runners! The effect is a good deal more funny than the humour of a profes-sional humorist, for it has that essential ingredient of real humour, unexpectedness; and he who does not laugh at first sight of the peas among those amazing popples, and the boats amid the beans, must be a dull dog.

Some 25 years later, in an article from the *Western Morning News* of 18 May 1932, Budleigh Salterton is described as follows:

Successfully resisting tendencies towards modernizing and popularizing, Budleigh Salterton has retained throughout the peculiar charm, which has made it one of the most delightful of the East Devon watering-places... During the past winter the principal hotels have been quite well patronized, and many visitors, attracted by the 'Winter at home' campaign, were agreeably surprised at the mildness of the climate and the general

amenities of their surroundings. These advantages are proving a growing inducement to people to settle down in Budleigh Salterton, and steady and attractive building development is in progress. A number of pleasant dwellings of the villa type have been erected on the outskirts of Budleigh Salterton of late years, but by reason of its compact position and layout these add to, rather than, detract from, the charm of the town, and 'ribbon' development, which mars the approaches to many resorts, has been avoided.

It is also mentioned that Mr Kerslake, the secretary of the Chamber of Commerce, had informed the paper that a throng of intending visitors and prospective residents, some of whom lived in India, had been making enquires about Budleigh Salterton. It appears the latter had been recommended to move to Devon upon retirement.

The Modern-Day Town

Many would say that Budleigh Salterton has changed little during the course of the twentieth century. One thing is for sure, the town has not been 'vulgarised' over the years: it has remained much as various writers have described it, although the population has increased, necessitating the building of more accommodation. Of course nowadays cars are everywhere, and may be considered to blight the town, especially in relation to the main street. Nevertheless, Budleigh Salterton remains a pleasant place, untainted by the arcades and bingo halls so apparent in many seaside towns.

What has changed about Budleigh Salterton is the manner in which it is referred to. Walter Scutt sets the background for this in his 1936 publication *East Budleigh & Hayes Barton*, where he states:

It seems a pity that the simple name BUDLEY should have been ousted by EAST BUDLEIGH, and similarly that the distinctive old name SALTERTON should be cumbered with its superfluous modern prefix.

Budleigh Salterton is now commonly referred to as Budleigh – the former name for East Budleigh – and this not just by the young but the elderly also.

References:
K. Batten and F. Bennett, 'The Printed Maps of Devon', *County Maps 1575–1837* (Tiverton, Devon Books, 1996).
British Medical Council, *A Book of the South West* (Exeter & London, Pollard & Co, 1907).
T.N. Brushfield, MD, 'Notes of the Parish of East

Budleigh', *Transactions Devonshire Association* (1890) vol.22; (1894) vol.26; 'The Church of All Saints, East Budleigh Part', *Transactions Devonshire Association* (1890) vol.22; (1892) vol.24.

R. Butler, (ed.) *A View from the Cliffs – The East Devon Heritage Coast* (Tiverton, Devon Books, 1986).

H.C. Darby and R. Welldon Finn (eds.), *The Domesday Geography of South-West England* (London, Cambridge University Press, 1967).

Devon County Archaeology Service, *Ancient Sites and Monuments Register* (Also telephone discussion between B. Horner and myself over evidence of saltpans in Budleigh Salterton, 13 May 2003).

Devon Records Office: Swete, *Devon Tour* (1792–1801) vol.10, 96M/Box 38/4; Sacrament Certificates 1748 QS/21/1748/3, DR5/698.

M. Duffy, S. Fisher, B. Greenhill, D.J. Starkey, J. Youings (eds), *The New Maritime History of Devon: From Early Times to the Eighteenth Century* (London, University of Exeter, 1992) vol.1; *The New Maritime History of Devon: From the Late Eighteenth Century to the Present Day* (London, University of Exeter, 1994) vol.2.

J.R., *Devon and Cornwall Notes and Queries* (1975) vol.33.

T. Gray (ed.), *The Traveller's East Devon* (Exeter, The Mint Press, 2000).

C.G. Harper, *The South Devon Coast* (London, Chapman and Hall, 1907).

H. Haseler, *Scenery on the Southern Coast of Devonshire* (Sidmouth, J. Wallis, 1818).

R. Polewhele, *The History of Devonshire,* (Dorking, Kohler & Coombes, 1977) vols. 2/3.

P. Salway, *Roman Britain* (Oxford, The Folio Society, 1985).

C. & F. Thorn (eds.), *Domesday Book: Devon, Parts 1 & 2* (Chichester, Phillimore, 1985).

Trewman's *Exeter Flying Post*.

G.T. Warner, *Landmarks in English Industrial History* (London, Blackie, 1908).

R. Welldon Finn, *Domesday Book: A Guide* (Chichester, Phillimore, 1973).

Westcountry Studies Library: various newspaper cuttings.

White's *Directory of Devon,* 1850 (New York, A.M. Kelly, 1968).

The Britannia Hotel, Knowle, c.1951.

(STEVE RICHARDSON)

Chapter 2

◇

Budleigh Haven

The mouth of the River Otter, c.1910.

(STEVE RICHARDSON)

Many of Devon's tidal river mouths enjoyed maritime trade during medieval times. Over the years, however, access to the smaller ports of Devonshire became obstructed by shingle. Budleigh Haven, was one such port.

Prior to this, probably from about the late-Neolithic period of 3000BC onwards, Budleigh Salterton was evidently thought to have been a good landing-place for boats. Shipping movement along the South Coast, emanating from trade in stone tools and pots, may well have made use of landing-places on the south coast of Devon, either as planned breaks or simply for refuge when stormy weather appeared on the horizon.

The relatively small port at the mouth of the River Otter was a 'tide haven', i.e. vessels had to rely on the tide to negotiate entry into the port. Over the years this haven was also commonly known as 'Ottermouth' and 'Ottermouth Haven', but for the sake of consistency it will be referred to as Budleigh Haven throughout this chapter, with the exception of quotations which may sometimes contain the other names.

Prominent Devonshire Ports

The riverside port of Topsham acted as the outport

for Exeter whose own port had been eliminated from maritime trade in the middle of the thirteenth century. The Courtenay family had built weirs across the river, preventing ships from reaching the city, and merchants, therefore, had to unload their cargoes at Topsham.

Of the smaller Devonshire ports Teignmouth was the most renowned during the thirteenth and fourteenth centuries. The decline of Teignmouth was due to its shallow harbour, competition from ports such as Exeter and Dartmouth, as well as the presence of ships from smaller ports such as Budleigh Haven. A French raid in 1340 would also have contributed to its downfall. Budleigh Haven also suffered from the lack of a deep port, with trade being confined to coastal activity and fishing which probably engaged the greatest portion of labouring people along the coast.

The Devonshire Fleet

During the years 1324–1402, five ships from the port of Budleigh Haven made up one per cent of Devon's fleet of ships in royal service; Exmouth, by contrast, had 34 ships.

In 1342 Sir Walter de Mauny was dispatched to Brittany with a large fleet. Budleigh Haven was to supply a small rowing vessel, known as a barge, for what was probably intended as a second fleet. It seems, however, that along with other vessels from Sidmouth, Teignmouth and Exmouth, the Budleigh Haven barge did not bother to join the second fleet.

With regards to trading vessels, Budleigh Haven had one wine boat at Bordeaux during the years 1372–86; this formed just half a per cent of the total of Devon's fleet. Exmouth had ten boats at Bordeaux. During the period 1340–1408 Devon's fleet consisted of 187 boats; 11 of these were from Budleigh Haven, totalling six per cent of the fleet. Of these 11 boats, two were owned by individual Budleigh residents. In comparison, Exmouth had 18 boats in Devon's fleet during this time.

The River Otter at Budleigh Salterton, c.1960. (STEVE RICHARDSON)

Banks of the River Otter, 1920s. (STEVE RICHARDSON)

Cottages at Granary, c.1920. (STEVE RICHARDSON)

Medieval Budleigh Haven

Tithes testify to the importance of fishing around the coast of East Devon: Sidmouth and Otterton fish tithes were worth more than £13 in the year 1408. During the latter part of the eleventh century Exeter enforced its rights over the Exe estuary whereby:

men of East Budleigh Hundred accused Exeter officials in the king's eyre court of hindering them from purchasing fish and other cargoes at Exmouth as they once had been able to do so.

As an example of other cargoes at Budleigh Haven, the Exeter cathedral works paid to cart iron from Budleigh Haven to Exeter in the 1330s.

A Petition to the King

Budleigh Haven played a significant part in the war between King Edward III and his neighbour across the English Channel. Calais, 'one of the strongest and richest of the French Channel ports', was captured on 4 August 1347. As a result the French took revenge against the English. One event in particular was to have calamitous repercussions: the French captured three ships and 12 boats from East Budleigh, carrying a total of 141 men. After this event, the people of 'Buddelegh' sent a petition to King Edward III, pleading for lower taxes to compensate for this great loss:

That whereas the said people are charged with the constant watch upon the sea against the enemies of our said Lord the King, and also the said poor people are destroyed by the said enemies, who have taken from the said town upon the sea three ships and twelve boats, in which ships and boats were one hundred and forty-one men of the richest merchants and mariners of the said town since Easter last past; of whom some were killed, others taken and imprisoned, some ransomed, and the others remaining in prison, have nothing wherewith to pay their ransom by reason that their goods were so taken from them; the which people thus killed, taken, and imprisoned, and thus deprived of their goods were wont to pay the greater part of the tenths* of the said town, wools, and other collections granted to our Lord the King: and the others who were left have been so grievously distrained and charged by the collectors of the tenths and wools aforesaid that some of them are begging, and the others are on the point of quitting their lands and tenements, so that the people aforesaid cannot in any way pay the said tenths and wools according to the assessment made upon them before this time, as

* A tax, comprising one-tenth of an individual's income, paid to the church.

more fully is found by an Inquiry taken by virtue of a Commission made thereon by the Council of our said Lord the King upon their grievous plaint, and returned into Chancery, whereby the said people pray that it may please his Majesty in his mercy to command the Chancellor that upon the said Inquiry returned before him, the said poor people may be taxed in such a way that they may not be altogether destroyed.

As a result of the petition an inquisition was held on 28 November 1347. John de Ralegh of Beaudeport (Aylesbeare), Richard de Brauncecombe (Branscombe) and Thomas de Holbrok (Clyst Honiton), were given the following orders:

Having arrived at the said town you shall survey it, and the state of the men of the same, in order to have better information thereupon.

The inquisition must have proved favourable to the people of 'Buddelegh' as the decision of the Council was as follows:

It seems to the Council, if it please the King, that it would be a great mercy to diminish the tax, by reason of such great and horrible destruction made of the people and ships of the same town, as it is found by the Inquiry taken thereon by the Commission of the King, and returned into Chancery. And by reason of such great destruction it [the Council] is of accord that they should have respite from the demand made upon them by wools and tenths until the Close of Easter [i.e. the first after Easter], so that in the meantime they may proceed towards the King in order to have his good will in the matter.

At the time of the seizure of the Budleigh ships small Devonshire towns were producing wool, much of which was exported to the Continent. The ships which carried the wool on the outward journey returned with wine and other products. Doubtless many cargoes of wool were shipped from Budleigh Haven to the Continent and it would probably have been on a return voyage that the ships and men of Budleigh, along with their merchandise, were captured.

Whilst the petition demonstrates that the loss of ships, boats and men was a severe blow to the mercantile community of Budleigh, it also indicates that the mid-fourteenth-century Budleigh Haven was quite an important port for its size. Hoskins, however, insists that although smaller ports such as Budleigh Haven 'could produce a ship or two for military expeditions [...] their commercial importance was trifling'. Doubtless those who were attacked by the French in 1347 would not concur.

Boats on the River Otter, c.1960. (NICK LOMAN COLLECTION)

The Decline of Budleigh Haven

In 1565 there was close administrative control over foreign trade. In order to minimise custom evasion, lists were drawn up of all the harbours, creeks and other places where goods might be traded; records known as Port Books were also kept. Budleigh Haven is no longer listed as a harbour by this time. An explanation for this fact is offered by Leland, writing c.1538, when he refers to the River Otter as:

a mere trout-stream... Ships of small burthen enter the mouth; but the bar is long, shallow and winding.

Leland goes on to describe the fate of the port as follows:

Less than one hundred years ago, ships used this haven... but it is now clean barred. Some call this haven Budleigh Haven of Budleigh Town.

Although small ships could enter the mouth of the river, the haven could no longer be used by vessels of any substantial size; it had become choked with silt.

In 1553 Richard Duke, who had purchased former monastic land on either side of the River Otter, received contributions that originated from a most unusual source towards 'the costs of making a haven at Ottermouth' (i.e. Budleigh Haven). These contributions were not, however, used to pay for the

removal of sand and silt from the mouth of the river; Duke had planned a much grander solution.

In the British Library there is a detailed map, dating from c.1540, belonging to the collection of Lord Burghley. Part of the map shows the south-east coast of Devon, with the havens of Dartmouth, Teignmouth, Exmouth and Ottermouth (i.e. Budleigh Haven). Exeter, (East) Budleigh, Otterton, Sidmouth and Seaton are all represented by illustrations of churches. At the mouth of the River Otter is a sailing ship; three other ships are situated upriver. The area of the map showing Exmouth and Budleigh Haven seems to be of a much larger scale than that used to show the coastline at Brixham and Dartmouth. Moreover, to the entrance of the mouth of the Otter lie two exaggerated projections. These projections were part of:

an Elizabethan scheme for a massive stone-walled channel protruding from the river mouth, providing access for ships to a haven large enough to dwarf that of the Exe.

To what extent the situation at Budleigh Haven improved is not known. The jetties were never constructed and any clearing of the silted-up river mouth would only have been of an ephemeral nature, if it had taken place at all.

As for the contributions received by Richard Duke, they came from the Church. During the reign of Edward VI, a commission was set up in 1549 to

Nick and Rob Loman with other boys on the River Otter, 1954. (NICK LOMAN COLLECTION)

'enquire into the quantity and value of church furniture throughout England, and to forbid their sale or misappropriation'. Three years later, another commission investigated those church goods appearing in the inventories of 1549 to see if they had, after all, been sold or misappropriated. It is from the records of this second commission that we find that Richard Duke had benefited from Sidmouth, Otterton and East Budleigh churches. The inquiry for the Hundred of East Budleigh shows:

Parochia de Sydmouth.
Also one bell the value of xli [£10] omyttyd out of the last Inventory and nowe presented by the parisshens their which bell was geven by the parisshens to Mr Richard Duke towardes the makyng of Ottermouth Haven and the same bell was bought of him by Mr. Raleigh for xli which matter is also referred to the Kynges mates Councell.

Parochia de Otterton.
One bell the value of [?] which the parisshens their gave to Mr Duke before the last certificath made towardes the makyng of the haven of Ottermouth which matter is also referred to the Kynges mates Councell.

Parochia de Estbudlegh.
One bell their specified in the last certificath was geven to Mr Duke by the seid parisshens towardes the makyng of Ottermouth Haven Also one Crosse of sylver was sold by the parisshens befere the makyng of the last certificath for xlvli [£45] wherof they gave to Mr Duke xxvli [£25] towardes the makyng of the seid haven of Ottermouth And the rest they bought a pece of ordynaunce called a Slynger for the defence of the country their which cost xxli [£20] and the same pece of ordynaunce is nowe in the Custody of the maire of exeter which matter is also referred to the Kynges mates Councell.

Why church property should have been donated to Richard Duke for the clearance and possible enlargement of Budleigh Haven, referred to here as 'Ottermouth Haven', can only be pondered upon.

Local Shipwrights

In 1513 Henry VIII used skilled shipwrights and caulkers from different parts of Devon to construct his ship *Henry Grace à Dieu* and three galleys at Woolwich. Amongst them were five impressed men from Otterton.

East Budleigh and Otterton were not without this class of artisan. The construction of ships around the coast of Devon was often a family effort, requiring no more than a waterside site and locally produced tools. Perhaps the greatest difficulty faced by a shipwright during these times would have been setting aside the money to purchase a stock of seasoned timber.

One such shipwright was William Smyth from East Budleigh. Upon his death in 1623, he left 'two saws and his working tools' to his son John. The family home was shared with William's daughter

Pew bench end, East Budleigh church, depicting a ship on the high seas. (AUTHOR)

and her husband, who was also a shipwright. William must have had a smallholding as he also left his son four sheep, as well as a hook, hatchet, mattock and shovel. The shipbuilding business must therefore have been quite small, as William needed to supplement his living by working the smallholding. This is corroborated by the value of his estate which was computed at a mere £22.3d.

William Bayley of Otterton was of more substantial worth. Upon his death in 1613 his estate was valued at £107.14s.8d.

Another Otterton shipwright, John Bayley (who may well have been William's brother), seems to have been a shipbuilder of some consequence. His name appears on Trinity House certificates for newly built ships sent to London for armaments between 1625 and 1638. In fact, out of three ships from Dartmouth, two from Exeter and one from Plymouth, John had built all but one, including the 140-ton *Resolution* of Exeter, and the *Merchant Royal* of Dartmouth. John died in 1638, but the family continued to build ships until the 1650s.

Churchwardens' Accounts

Churchwardens' accounts are often a useful source of information for those researching the past. The accounts for 1664, for example, show that £2.12s. was paid for 'ii boates lade of Stones att [Budleigh] havenmouth' and a further £1.16s.8d for the 'carrige of the saide stone from bancley to the churchyard'. This entry reveals that boats laden with stones were able to navigate their way up to Bankly, situated on the west side of the river mouth. The Ordnance Survey map of 1938 (scale: 6in to 1 mile) shows the 'Highest Point to which Ordinary tides flow' as lying just above Bankly, thus indicating that perhaps any boat going up the river would need a high tide to reach its destination.

Over 100 years later, the churchwardens' accounts of 1778 show that a sum of 2s. was paid to a 'Mr Bartlett for his Boat to bringing of Stones', and 5s. for 'Drawing the same from Bankly'.

Lord Rolle's Embankment

The Ordnance Survey map of 1891 shows an embankment commencing from Granary and heading in a northerly direction on the west side of the river, past Otterton Park, until it reaches the point to which the highest tides flow; it then curves towards the west and then back towards Bankly. Another smaller embankment continues on from the point where the main embankment curves west-

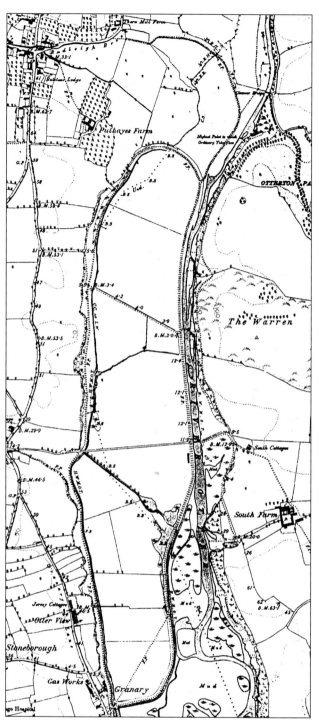

The 1891 Ordnance Survey map (scale: 6in to 1 mile; reduced) showing the embankments that had been constructed by Lord Rolle along the River Otter.

(CLINTON DEVON ESTATES)

wards; it continues northwards along the west bank of the river, before curving to the west and terminating opposite Thorn Mill farm. These embankments were created by Lord Rolle in 1812 and reclaimed in all about 160 acres of land. This development was not, however, always seen in a positive light and was later deemed responsible for the loss of the harbour.

'Gent' Mears making crab pots on Budleigh Salterton beach, 1960s. (NICK LOMAN COLLECTION)

Fisherman Harry Rogers, 1930s. (NICK LOMAN COLLECTION)

This photograph is thought to show members of the Sedgemore family, 1930s. (NICK LOMAN COLLECTION)

Fishermen offloading their net from a donkey cart at the bottom of the lane that runs onto the beach from the Temple Methodist Church, 1890s.

(NICK LOMAN COLLECTION)

The Two Sisters, *late 1800s. There were 107 boats registered for fishing at Budleigh Salterton during this time. This figure included one-man boats.*

(NICK LOMAN COLLECTION)

The negative impact of the embankment upon the harbour was discussed at a public meeting held at the Rolle Arms Inn, Budleigh Salterton, in April 1858. The aim of this meeting was to re-organise the Committee of Public Works and Improvements, and at the same time to discuss whether or not the 'harbour question' should be reopened. J. Holmes JP presided, whilst the principal speakers were C. Harris (chairman), J. Thawite and C. Wescomb.

During the course of the meeting it was alleged that the consequences of erecting the embankment, were as follows:

[Ships had been] prevented from proceeding as far as Otterton Bridge, where they had previously been in the habit of discharging their cargoes, and the poor fisherman had been deprived of an honest livelihood.

The embankment, it was said, had manufactured the natural harbour to uselessness. Moreover, lives had not only been put in jeopardy, but had already been sacrificed. The tide, on being thwarted from reaching the marshy land, 'produced a rental, claimed and secured by the trustees of the late lord's estate'. It was stated that guns had been taken away from sportsmen whilst 'others had been fined by the magistrates for trespassing and killing wild fowl'.

Eight years earlier, in 1850, Captain Washington had been sent by the Admiralty to investigate the effects of the embankment on the mouth of the Otter. He concluded that:

the inhabitants might destroy the embankment, and declared that he would indemnify them from any legal proceedings which Lord Rolle's trustees might take against them.

Calling upon Lord Rolle's trustees to restore the harbour had not, however, proved successful. The meeting at the Rolle Arms Inn had therefore been called to determine which course of action should be taken. Of course it was also a prime opportunity for the locals to vent their anger:

the act of Lord Rolle in making the embankment was described in very harsh terms, and it was complained that the Hon. Mark Rolle could never be seen in their neighbourhood, and that he had not taken any measure to do justice to the town.

Three possible courses of action were established: they could either petition the Hon. Mark Rolle and the late Lord Rolle's trustees to restore the harbour; failing that they could appeal to the Admiralty or to the Attorney-General. After much discussion, the consensus was to follow the first course of action. A petition was presented to the Hon. Mark Rolle and the late Lord Rolle's trustees requesting that measures be taken to:

restore the harbour to its original state, or by a pier or otherwise make the river a safe harbour for boats of the burthen accustomed to frequent the river and harbour prior to the embankment being made which has caused the obstruction.

It was agreed that if the trustees and the Hon. Mark Rolle did not acquiesce to the inhabitant's wishes, they would turn to the Admiralty.

On 21 May 1858 the Sidmouth antiquarian, Peter Orlando Hutchinson, wrote the following about the Budleigh Salterton encroachments in his diary:

the inhabitants of Budleigh Salterton have recently been loudly complaining of the injury done to the harbour by the Rolle family for twenty or thirty years past, by enclosing some of the flats and thereby curtailing the size of the basin… about thirty acres of land had been enclosed.

Locals had informed him that before the enclosure of the flats, the rising tide had swept in large quantities of water which rushed out when the tide fell, thus keeping the river mouth open and securing a deep channel. Unfortunately, this was no longer the case:

since these encroachments have been made the channel and the mouth have been filled up. When the tide was only two hours up from low water, boats [...] could enter, whereas now they can only enter when the water is nearly high.

The contents of a letter dating from 25 September 1858 headed 'The Lost Budleigh Harbour' reveal that the trustees and the Hon. Mark Rolle had ignored the entreaty of the Budleigh Salterton people. Once again the Admiralty had become involved in the dispute. On 11 May 1858 naval engineer W.S. Andrews (author of the letter) and Rear-Admiral Bullock, admiralty surveyor, made an 'eye survey' of the River Otter. After inspecting the estuary and outfall of the River Otter at noon and at low tide they observed the following:

the mouth of the river was confined between a bed of rocks on the east side, and a high shingle beach on the west; the stream at the narrowest part being about

thirty yards across, and with about two feet of water in the deepest part. Further out the water fell over a bed of shingle in a rapid stream, and had about one foot of water. Within the shingle beach the river divided itself into two streams – one turning suddenly to the west, the other continuing its course in a northerly direction. Between the streams a flat of about twenty acres, partly dry at high water, extends for a distance of about four hundred yards, where a dyke or embankment crosses the western arm of the river, and stretching away in a north easterly direction, encloses about sixty acres of land, formerly the estuary of the river, and which supplied the large quantity of back water that nature required to keep the mouth of the harbour open.

This account is followed by that of James Webber, an 80-year-old fisherman, reminiscing in c.1860. His recollections lend weight to the accusation that the embankment had indeed had a negative impact on the harbour:

[He] stated that he remembered the river from his boyhood, and at that time the mouth was so wide that vessels of sixty tons could work in [it]; and that he himself was master of a vessel that traded in the harbour, and had often discharged his cargo as far up as the upper salmon pool, where there was twelve to fourteen feet of water, and fish in great abundance were caught there. That the harbour continued in this state until about fifty years ago, or in about 1810, when, for the purpose of enclosing a piece of land, a bank was

Herring catch, 1900s. (NICK LOMAN COLLECTION)

41

commenced to be made, and a very large quantity – thousands and thousands of tons – of rock was taken away from the east side of the entrance; and through depriving the river of this large surface of back water, and taking away the ground and rock on the east side, and thus allowing the water to escape in that direction, the entrance soon became blocked up, and gradually came into the state in which it now is.

The elderly fisherman was adamant that the embankment was to blame. As proof of this he continues:

in the year 1824, in the great gale, the sea broke through the dyke, and allowed the water to flow over the enclosed space, when the effect of the back water was such that in about a fortnight the harbour was nearly as good as ever, and continued so until they repaired the dyke, upon which the harbour returned to its former and present state. [He further stated that] the piece of land enclosed is three feet below the level of the sea at high water; [and he is certain that] it only requires to open the dyke, and allow the water to return to its former bed, to restore the entrance and harbour to their previous good state.

Several other fishermen and residents corroborated his story. Andrews concludes that man was indeed to blame for the loss of the harbour, and made no bones about revealing which particular man he deemed responsible:

It can be seen at a glance by any practical man that here are the ruins of a natural harbour, destroyed by the agency of man, and that had nature been left undisturbed by her own wise laws, the harbour would have been kept open for centuries as it had been for ages before. There can be no doubt that this act was unjusti[fi]able; that it was done for personal aggrandizement, to the loss and injury of the crown, the local inhabitants, and the nation at large, as well as the ultimate injury of the descendants of the aggressor. Now sir, if they will take my advice, they will at once cause an inquiry to be made into the facts with a view to its restitution, for the length of time that has elapsed only adds to the injury inflicted on the nation, and does not lessen the claim of the crown. Let the descendants of Lord Rolle do this from a sense of justice, instead of being compelled, as they ultimately must be, to give up what they had no right to take, and by this act of justice earn fame and renown instead of being accused of having done wrong for the sake of a few paltry acres of land they do not want, for surely Providence has been bountiful to them in this respect, already possessing as they do one of the most fertile and beautiful valleys on earth. I have yet to see the future Lord Rolle's yacht all

'ataunt' in the harbour he will restore, eh! And his gunboat Sun *manned by his own tenantry to defend, if need be the bountiful possessions Providence has been pleased to bestow upon him.*

It would appear that some had questioned the motives for Andrews's conclusion. In a letter dated 11 October 1858 and published in a newspaper (it is not known which) he vociferously defended himself:

I beg respectively… to repudiate all political feeling or motive… The object of my remarks, accompanying the report of the survey, was to call the attention of the owners of Bicton to the injury that had been done to the resident population, the nation and themselves… after mature enquiry and consideration have been given to this important subject, they may be induced, either by feelings of justice and right, or by self interest (the strongest of all human agencies) to restore to the inhabitants, and to the nation at large, that which they have so unfairly deprived them of... surely they cannot compare the value of a few acres of marsh land to the profit and advantages of a fine harbour, a thriving trade, a populous and fashionable town, and a happy and contented population… I shall be happy to render them any assistance my experience may afford with a view to its restoration…

All recommendations made by Andrews went unheeded. Whether he was actually correct in concluding that the construction of the embankment had caused water loss in the Otter is open to speculation; the same must be said of his remedy, i.e. the removal of the embankment, as this was not put to the test.

Nevertheless, during an inquest held in Budleigh Salterton 30 years earlier on 1 January 1828, jurors had clearly deemed the embankment to be responsible for the following unfortunate incident. On 13 December 1827 the mariner William Gibbs, aged about 26 years, drowned with his father whilst attempting to run ashore. The jury returned the following verdict:

That the said William Gibbs, on the 13th day of December, in the year of our Lord, 1827, being in a boat off Budleigh Salterton aforesaid, the weather being stormy, the said boat accidentally upset, and the said William Gibbs, together with his father, Joseph Gibbs aged about 70 years was then and there drowned; and it is the opinion of the Jurors, that if the harbour at Budleigh Salterton had been as it was about 18 years ago, and before the enclosure by Lord Rolle of the land which then formed the bed of the river, the deceased would have been able to have entered the harbour with his boat in safety.

Herrings being packed for transportation to Billingsgate Market, 1900s.
(NICK LOMAN COLLECTION)

Fishermen on the beach, 1900s.
(STEVE RICHARDSON)

Mackerel fishing at Budleigh Salterton, 1900s.
(NICK LOMAN COLLECTION)

Baiting crab pots, c.1950. (Nick Loman Collection)

The jurors' verdict, which substantiates the claim made at the meeting in April that 'lives had been sacrificed,' may also absolve to a degree Andrews's determination to blame the embankment for the silting up of the river mouth. Doubtless though, natural occurrences over a period of many years also contributed to the loss of the Otter as a natural haven. This phenomenon has occurred in many a river up and down the country.

Plans for a Sea Wall

In 1863, five years on from Andrews's attempt to reinstate the Otter harbour, the estuary was inspected again. Nicholas Whitley of Truro wanted to create a harbour for fishing boats and yachts, rather than large vessels. A tideway was to be fabricated, with a pebble ridge forming a wall behind which boats could shelter.

Whitley reported that a growing shingle bank had impeded the entrance of the harbour, only leaving a narrow channel on the eastern side of the estuary. Large amounts of shingle had accumulated and the width of the bank had doubled. The shingle tended to move eastward and had choked up the old mouth of the river, forcing it to form a new channel to the east. The shingle thrown into the new channel by the surf was in turn washed out to sea by the river 'freshes', thus forming a bank across the new channel.

He concluded that the creation of a harbour would cost a substantial amount of money which simply could not be justified due to the small amount of sea-going traffic in the area. He recommended, however, that the following work should be undertaken:

That in order to prevent the Travelling of the Shingle into and beyond the Channel, a sea wall be constructed along the eastern crest of the Shingle Bank and across the old channel to the ledge of rocks marked in Red… on the plan. This wall might be constructed by the materials now on the spot. The large rocks at the foot of the Cliff… should be placed unhewn to form the base of the wall across the old Channel, and the insterstices [sic] filled, and the remainder of the wall completed with Shingle grouted with blue lias lime having a slope of 4 and 5 to 1 outside and 3 to 1 inside and made 5 feet wide at the Top. This would effactually prevent the Shingle from being washed into the Channel, and as the sea throws up additional Shingle on the slope of the wall it might be grouted and retained so as further to protect the Channel. The ledge of Rocks would prevent any further shingle from being gathered at the mouth of the new Channel… and with South West and westerly winds boats could pull up under the lee of these rocks and reach Harbour in comparatively still water. Some of the rocks in the new Channel will require to be blown up and removed, and the Channel should be cleared of Shingle and deepened at one or two places.

Whitley estimated the cost of this work as being somewhere between £500 and £600.

The Hon. Mark Rolle and Lord Coleridge, riparian owners, were sent copies of Whitley's report.

There is no indication as to whether the work was actually carried out.

A small harbour was, however, made by fishermen, as the *Devon and Exeter Gazette* reported in 1886:

The gales from the south east that have been prevailing for some time have unfortunately washed in such a bank of pebbles that the entrance to the little harbour at the mouth of the Otter is entirely blocked. The fishermen took infinite pains to make this harbour a year or two since. Previous to this on many days suitable for fishing they were obliged to remain idle owing to surf on the beach which is a very bad one for landing.

By 1892, the silting up of the river mouth had worsened to the extent that even ordinary fishing boats were unable to enter it.

The Otter Mouth Improvement Committee

In 1928 another harbour scheme was proposed. At a quarterly meeting of the Devon Sea Fisheries Committee, held in Newton Abbot in January 1928, the formation of a private committee was reported: the Otter Mouth Improvement Committee. Working with the full consent of Lord Clinton and his agent, the committee had undertaken surveys and soundings with a view to building a harbour. This was, of course, good news for fisherman who, since the silting up of the river mouth, had been forced to land their catches on the shingle in the surf. A circular asking for donations had been issued; they also hoped to raise debentures to fund the scheme, with the promoters forming a club and asking other people to become members. As with the previous good intentions, nothing came of this proposal.

The Modern-Day Landscape

With its source within the Blackdown Hills situated on the Devon–Somerset border, the Otter lends its name to many places as it makes its short journey down to the sea at Budleigh Salterton. The crest of the embankment constructed by Lord Rolle to drain the area now forms a convenient footpath alongside the Otter; there is no longer any visible trace of the haven that was to our forefathers not merely part of the landscape but vital to their everyday life. How many of those people alighting from their vehicles at the Lime Kiln car park and setting off along the River Otter actually know about the history of the haven? Once on the pathway, look ahead, slightly to the left and you will see the South Farm cottages. These cottages, accessed from the main Budleigh Salterton to East Budleigh road, at the junction with Granary Lane and South Farm, mark the limits of the harbour basin that once constituted the haven.

A view from Lime Kiln car park, looking towards Granary up to South Farm Cottages from the footpath, an area that was once 'Budleigh Haven', 2004. (AUTHOR)

A view from South Farm Cottages looking towards Otterton Point, 2004. (AUTHOR)

Budleigh Haven – Facts and Figures

John Helyer – *Helyer* meaning roofer – of Budleigh Haven is mentioned as importing a cargo of roofing slates in 1367/8.

Henry V used Devon ships as part of his fleet in 1417, with Dartmouth sending four, Budleigh Haven five, and Brixham and Barnstaple one.

Budleigh Haven supplied a ship to convey troops for Henry VI, during the period 1439–1452.

When the *James* of Budleigh Haven was at the port of London in 1474, Harry Denys failed to load the ship within five days as had been agreed. The ship's owner, Matthew Andrew, sued Denys.

Upon the threat of the Spanish Armada in July 1570, Budleigh mustered 16 mariners.

In 1595 Parliament decreed that vessels should be 'manned, armed, and victualled' by the ports at local charge. Exeter was required to provide four vessels at this time but pleaded poverty so the 'creeks and limbs' (i.e. small rivers supporting trading or naval boats) which included Budleigh Haven, were notified to assist the city.

In a survey of 1619, 168 shipwrights were consolidated in three main locations across Devon consisting of Dartmouth, Plymouth and, perhaps unexpectedly, Otterton, with 21 shipwrights.

References:

J. Butler (ed.), *Travels in Victorian Devon – Illustrated Journals and Sketchbooks 1846–1870 of Peter Orlando Hutchinson* (Tiverton, Devon Books, 2000).

T.N. Brushfield, MD, 'Notes of the Parish of East Budleigh', *Transactions Devonshire Association* (1890) vol.22, (1894) vol.26 ; 'The Church of All Saints, East Budleigh', *Transactions Devonshire Association* (1890) vol.22, (1892) vol.24.

E.A.G. Clark, *The Ports of the Exe Estuary 1660–1860* (Exeter, The University of Exeter, 1960).

Devon Record Office: 96M/Box 38/4.

M. Duffy, S. Fisher, B. Greenhill, D.J. Starkey, J. Youings (eds.), *The New Maritime History of Devon: From Early Times to the Eighteenth Century* (London, University of Exeter, 1992) vol.1, and *From the Late Eighteenth Century to the Present Day* (London, University of Exeter, 1994) vol.2.

M.G. Dickenson, (ed.), *Devon's Fishing Industry and its Fishermen* (Tiverton, Devon Books, 1987).

M.H. Keen, *History of England: England in the Later Middle Ages* (London, The Folio Society, 1997) vol.3.

M. Kowaleski, *Local Customs Accounts of the Port of Exeter* (Exeter, Devon and Cornwall Record Society New Series, 1993) vol.36; *Local Markets and Regional Trade in Medieval Exeter* (Cambridge, Cambridge University Press, 1995).

M.M. Oppenheim, *The Maritime History of Devon* (Exeter, The University of Exeter, 1968).

R. Polewhele, *The History of Devonshire* (Dorking, Kohler & Coombes, 1977) vols. 2/3.

Trewman's *Exeter Flying Post*.

Westcountry Studies Library: newspaper cuttings.

Chapter 3

Parish Administration

View of the west side, Budleigh Salterton, 1950s. (Nick Loman Collection)

Vestry Meetings

East Budleigh dealt with its own parochial business through Vestry meetings, as was the case with other parishes in England. The meetings were attended by the male ratepayers of the parish and resulted in the annual appointment of the overseer of the poor, surveyor of highways, churchwardens and constables. Vestry meetings originated from Tudor times and were replaced in 1894 by the establishment of local councils.

Vestry meetings up and down the country were run by common law, each parish having its own interpretation of what that law should be. Impending meetings were advertised by a notice posted on the church door and signed by either the minister as residing incumbent or the churchwarden. The chairman of the meeting was the minister of the parish; if he was not present a chairman was elected by majority vote.

Minutes were taken at Vestry meetings and from these minutes we find that the business of the Vestry was manifold. The minutes of Vestry meetings generally followed a set pattern. The initial entry for each meeting related that a copy of the notice of the impending meeting had been posted on the church door. This was followed by a list of the ratepayers present and the name of the chairman. The business of the meeting was then entered as it took place. This included resolutions and whether they were passed, nominations for the various offices and those elected, as well as other decisions made during the meeting.

Extant minutes for East Budleigh cover the period 1857–71. Entries of interest from this book have been summarised below, grouped according to the official responsible for them. As the original minutes only report the discussion, it is therefore occasionally necessary to read between the lines in order to visualise exactly what happened.

Budleigh Salterton Town Band, 1930s. (NICK LOMAN COLLECTION)

The Octagon, 1920s. This is where Millais painted The Boyhood of Raleigh.
(STEVE RICHARDSON)

The Promenade, c.1910. (STEVE RICHARDSON)

The foreshore, 1930s. (STEVE RICHARDSON)

In addition to the Vestry minutes, information can be gleaned from the account books kept by the various officials. These books are rich in content and allow much insight into the social conditions of the day, especially in relation to the poor.

The Office of Churchwarden

Two churchwardens were normally appointed at Easter: one for the people, the other for the minister. Tait, in his book *The Parish Chest* (1946) informs us that an ecclesiastical authority defined churchwardens as 'the proper guardians or keepers of the parish church'. Certain nominees endeavoured to decline the office as it was often unsalaried. Until 1964, common law compelled any parishioner chosen as churchwarden to take up the office or be fined. On reading about some of the churchwardens' duties, however, it is quite easy to understand why people would rather pay a monetary penalty. The duties of the churchwardens included the following:

To manage parish property and income.
To represent the views of parishioners in parochial and collective matters.
The upkeep of the church fabric.
The provision of facilities for worship and the allocation of pews.
To encourage parishioners to attend church and to ensure children are baptised.
To attend the Archdeacon's court.
To account for the expenditure of the church rate.
To assist in the compilation of the parish register.
To supervise the education and relief of the poor in collaboration with the Overseers of the Poor.
To report if necessary any failing in the duty of the incumbent.
To maintain the parish arms and pay the local soldiers.
The control and extermination of vermin.
To present offences within the cognizance of the church courts.

The churchwardens' duties listed above are mostly of an ecclesiastical nature, but there are civil duties amongst them. At East Budleigh, one churchwarden was appointed 'for the land side' and 'one for the town', by which is meant the village of East Budleigh, not Budleigh Salterton.

The church rate collected by the churchwardens was levied on the amount of real property owned or leased; this compulsory payment was abolished in 1868. Church rates were not raised solely for the administration and upkeep of church fabric, they were put to multifarious uses. The diverse entries in the churchwardens' account books for East Budleigh show exactly how the money was spent, such as on repairs to the Parish Church, the relief of the so-called 'travelling poor' (who were travelling through the parish), on 'briefs' (a form of charity), as well as the control of vermin.

It must be stressed that the churchwardens' accounts and Vestry minute books date from the time before Budleigh Salterton was separated from East Budleigh and made a parish in its own right. During this period, the village of East Budleigh was the main focal point of the parish.

Church Expenses

In 1680, the church rate levied a sum of £9.8s. and the church burial of Mrs Pitfield raised an additional 6s.8d. The total receipts for the year amounted to £11.11s.8d.

Some of the disbursements made for the year in relation to the Parish Church included the following: wine for sacrament (22 quarts for the year cost £2, of which five quarts were consumed on Easter Day); 3s.6d. was spent on communion bread for the whole year and the washing of the table linen cost 1s.3d.; 1s.6d. was spent on 'Peter Pence' (a tenth-century tax imposed by the Pope); 1s.3d. covered the washing of the surplices.

Money spent on the church fabric included the following: 6s. for 'lyme to heal the church'; 2s.6d. covered the cost of shingles to repair the roof, plus a further 3s.6d. for lasts and nails, 8s.8d. for the workmen's wages, and a further 1d. for beer; 10s.6d. went on the 'glassing' of the church windows; 3s. was paid to Richard Callender and assistant for 'mending the floors in the church and lyme'; stakes for the churchyard hedge cost 2s.6d. whilst 1s.1d. was spent on 'iron work about the clock'; a rope for 'the little bell' cost 4s. and a further 1s.6d. was spent on 'collars for the bells'; the sum of 6d. bought a frame for the marriage table.

On 5 November 6s.2d. was paid to the bell-ringers (doubtless in observance of Bonfire Night). Another annual event, the beating of the parish bounds, cost 9s.6d.

Left: *Fore Street, 1900s.* (NICK LOMAN COLLECTION)

Below: *Fore Street looking towards the High Street, 1900s.* (STEVE RICHARDSON)

Fore Street, 1900s. The message on the back of this postcard, written by a visitor to Budleigh Salterton, reads: 'I am having a lovely time. I am writing this PC on Flagstaff. This morning I walked up over the cliffs and then down the Chine and back along the beach… the scenery is grand. I am having lovely weather with just one or two showers…'

(STEVE RICHARDSON)

Fore Street, 1900s. (STEVE RICHARDSON)

The churchwardens made four annual payments of £1.5s.4d. to cover 'gaol and hospital money'. Payments for 'taking out the transcript of Christenings Marriages and Burials' were 1s., whilst 6d. was paid for 'passing it in for the Bishop's register'. Making a church rate cost 6d., parchment for a bridge rate (authorised by an act of 1530–31) cost 4d. Expenses 'on ourselves and horses' amounted to 3s.6d. Taking miscellaneous expenses into account the churchwardens had a small shortfall on their hands at the end of the year, as the total sum expended (£11.17s.4d.) exceeded the annual income by 5s.8d.

In the year 1697, when expenditure did not exceed income, the balance of the account (10s.4d.) was spent 'in a dinner at Thomas Manfields' by the consent of the parishioners'. In 1702 the unspent church rates, a total of 11s.11½d., were put to much better use and donated to five poor people.

Expenses incurred over the years were many and varied: the weathercock had to be repaired, new glass was inserted in the windows of the church and when other repairs or alterations to the church building were carried out, money was also spent on beer for the workmen. In 1735 John Woodward received the sum of £14 for painting 'ye King's Arms and Ten Commandments' and making a frame for it.

Payments for events connected with the royal family during the seventeenth and eighteenth centuries include the following:

'Tolling' at the burial of the queen 1/-
Expenses for the kings [sic] coronation 13/-
Expenses for the kings [sic] birthday 3/-
Spent on the ringers on the kings [sic] birthday 2/6d
To be spent when the king is crowned 11/6d
For the ringers [at the] kings [sic] coronation 5/-
For the ringers on the birth of a princess 5/6d
For a thanksgiving prayer on the birth of a princess 1/-
For a prayer for the Prince of Wales 1/-

Victory in war also attracted notice. In 1761 money 'spent on the news for taking North America' amounted to 2s.6d. This was probably spent on a service of thanksgiving as the same sum was spent on a prayer and thanksgiving for Admiral Rodney's victory in April 1782 – the last important navel action in the American War of Independence.

As may be expected, rates were not always paid. In 1708 there were 'those that cannot nor are able to pay and will not' pay. This caused a deficiency of 14s.9d. for the year in question; whether this sum of money was ever recovered is not shown.

A Malt Money Rate, 1600

Stephen Awstine	vijd. [7d.]
John ffleye (Flay)	vijd. [7d.]
Gilberte Morren	iijs. [3s.]
Richard Hoppen	ijs. [2s.]
John Skarre	vijd. [7d.]
William Molle	ixd. [9d.]
Thomas Webber	xd. [10d.]
Elizabeth Leate widow	viijd. [8d.]
John fflowler (Flowler)	iijs. [3s.]
Edmond Mowdie	ijd. [2d.]
Richard Mowdye	ijd. [2d.]
Thomas Luccas	ijd. [2d.]
Walter Denis Esqr by Richard Hoppen	ijd. [2d.]

Parishioners of Salterton paid the above rate of malt money to the church of East Budleigh in 1600. Beer brewed in 'Church Houses' was sold in order to gain extra income towards defraying church expenses.

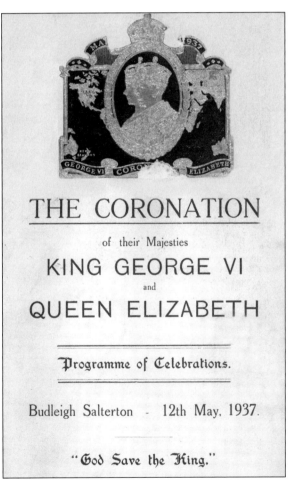

Programme for the coronation of King George VI and Queen Elizabeth on 12 May 1937.

(NICK LOMAN COLLECTION)

51

A celebratory parade, c.1920. (STEVE RICHARDSON)

Above and right: *A grand occasion at Queen's Street School, c.1920.* (STEVE RICHARDSON)

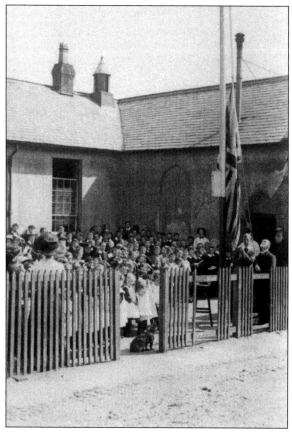

The Travelling Poor

Throughout the churchwardens' accounts are details of payments made to the poor passing through the parish. Many of these people were seaman or soldiers, or those who had been held captive in foreign parts and were just returning to their own place of settlement. These people should perhaps be classed as 'travellers' rather than being put into the category of the itinerant poor, but some of those receiving aid whilst traversing through East Budleigh were doubtless itinerants. The majority of the travellers are not classed by nationality so it is perhaps safe to assume they were British. Where listed, nationalities include French, Irish and Dutch, as well as one 'Garnsey' man and various Cornishmen. In 1664, four seamen with passes were given 1s., another seaman received 6d. for 'his lodging and supper', and during the course of the year a total of 1s.4d. was paid out to 14 Frenchmen.

The second Dutch war of 1665–67 was a period of time when the parish of East Budleigh contributed to the well-being of many injured soldiers. During the course of 1666, payments of 4s.6d. were made to four 'maimed' soldiers to cover the cost of lodgings and supper. Nine soldiers received 2s.4d, and 1s. was given to a 'lame soldier carried upon a horse'.

The hospitalisation of maimed soldiers cost 19s.6d., the highest payment made at this time. One soldier and his wife received 8d., another received 1s. for his wife and two children. Two seaman who had been taken prisoner by the Dutch received 1s.6d. for their supper and lodging.

In the year 1667 many of those passing through the parish had been taken captive. There were men and women 'taken by the Dutch', two seamen described as 'captives seven years', four woman with six children who had been 'taken at sea' and four seaman 'taken by the French'. There were also three seamen who had lost their ship at sea, and three Irish women with four children. A certain John Crosse received 2s.3d. 'for entertaining' two women i.e. giving them lodging and food. Similarly, a Richard Sayter was compensated in the sum of 1s. upon giving 'to an Irish woman in money and supper'. A sum of 3s. was shared amongst 13 poor people 'whome their houses were burnt having an order from Commissioners to travel from Cornwall'.

In 1668, payments were made to the following travellers: a man who had lost his ship at Harridge [Harwich]; two seaman who had been held prisoner in Holland; two women with three children from Kent; six French men who had been taken prisoner by the Spaniards and two women who had lost £900 in a fire.

Among the travellers during the year 1672 were

the following: 'a captain that lost his ship'; three seaman that 'came out of slavery'; two men that 'came out of Turkey'; six French men and four 'Irish folk'; 11 Scots who 'had lost by fire', nine Irish with 'a pass from the king', three men 'released out of Hollands prison', 'certain captives redeemed from Turkey', nine 'Frenchmen taken by the Hollanders' and four 'Cornishmen taken by ye Hollander'.

During 1673 a total of 100 travellers received money from the church rates. The next notable year for travellers was 1695 when their number included 24 soldiers from Flanders and a wounded drummer – they had probably served William III in the War of the League of Augsburg. Two seaman and their families were noted as having been 'taken by the French coming from the East Indies'. The sum of 1d. each was paid out to 11 soldiers from the East Indies, whilst a man with one leg, a wife and three children received 6d.

Two years later, in 1697, a total of 14 men 'taken by the French' and eight seaman also 'taken by the French' passed through the parish, as did 26 seaman returning from French prisons in 1712.

From 1697 onwards the account books show a remarkable drop in the number of travellers.

Vermin

An act of parliament in 1532–33 had the following consequences for vermin control:

In consequence of the innumerable number of rooks, crows and choughs, every parish, township, or hamlet, was to provide itself with a net for their destruction. Two pence was to be paid for every twelve old crows, rooks, or choughs, by the owner or the occupier of the manor or lands.

As seen from the list of churchwardens' duties earlier, we know they were the parish officials responsible for the control and extermination of vermin as specified by the act of 1532–33. We can only see evidence of payments from 1664 onwards, as the earliest extant churchwardens' account book dates from this year. It is plain that the East Budleigh churchwardens viewed pest control as a serious matter as throughout the years many entries record payments for the heads of various creatures. From the churchwardens' account books, an entry dated 15 February 1762 relates that:

Where as a parish meeting on Devouring Birds which are... Magpyes each head one penney Crowes Rookes and Choweses [choughs] and Jayes Kites and Hawks one penney each head and the Churchwardens agreed

Wisteria Cottages, 1950s. The library stands on this loca-tion in 2004. (NICK LOMAN COLLECTION)

upon this parrish Likewise for Sparrows and Upes [bullfinches] 2d per [dozen].

Shortly afterwards a payment of 6s.2d was made, which implies that at least 70 birds were killed at 1d. per bird. If, however, sparrows and bullfinches were the main target, at 2d. per dozen, then the total of dead birds would have been much greater.

The following year, 1763, must have been a particularly bad year for the so-called 'Devouring Birds': 320 were killed, resulting in a total payment of £1.6s.8d. The payments for dead birds differed somewhat from the previous year and were as follows: 2d. per kite; 1d. per jaie (jay); ½d. per upe or whoop (bullfinch); 1d. per chow (chough); 2d. per dozen sparrows.

Payments were made upon the head of the dead vermin being shown to the churchwardens. In the parish of East Budleigh, the following was also paid for certain animals: 1s. per fox; 1s. per gray (badger); 4d. per fitchew (weasel); 4d. per hedgehog; 4d. per mole.

Vermin – defined in the Concise Oxford Dictionary as 'mammals and birds injurious to game and crops e.g. foxes and rodents' – litter the East Budleigh churchwardens' account book. The *rattus rattus*, commonly known as the black, ship or house rat and the *rattus norvegicus*, the brown or common rat are, however, not to be found amongst the entries. The killing of hedgehogs and bullfinches may seem rather a repugnant act but it is not for us to judge our predecessors, especially as our knowledge of the habits of such animals is far greater today. Moreover, modern intensive farming methods have probably obliterated far greater numbers of birds than those destroyed for the purpose of crop protection at a time when agriculture was not so productive.

The following table shows payments made for vermin during 1664.

Vermin Payments for 1664	
John Chamon in town for 11 jays	11d.
Roger Smith 4 jays	4d.
Robert Condy 5 jays	5d.
John Burch for a kite	2d.
Mr Arscott's boy for a kite	2d.
John Burch for 9 jays	9d.
John Penswill 6 jays	6d.
John Leat's son Henry 4 jays	4d.
John Burch for 8 jays	8d.
George Cookny 4 jays	4d.
Roger Smith 2 jays	2d.
Isaac Clatworthy for 3 jays	3d.
Roger Smith 4 jays	4d.
John Burch 5 jays	5d.
William Mabill 6 jays	6d.
William Burch for a badger's head	1s.
George Lodden 6 jays	6d.
John Sharman in town for 4 jays	4d.
George [C]okney for 5 jays	5d.
Thomas Mansel 1 jay	1d.
Robert Brayne 3 jays	3d.
Mr Arscott for a kite	2d.
Ann Tucker 1 jay	1d.
Mr Arscott's boy 3 kites	6d.
Roger Smith 1 kite	2d.
Roger Smith 1 jay	1d.
Peter [Claye] for bullfinches	5d.
Ellis Coxe 2 badgers	2s.
William Burch for a badger's head	1s.
Peter [Claxe] for 2 jays and bullfinches	3d.
William Condy's son 1 kite	2d.
John Hooke 4 jays and 8 bullfinches	8d.

The amount paid by the churchwardens for the year totalled 14s.4d. for 170 heads, of which 158 were jays. Also of note is that a woman, Ann Tucker, appears in the list. She is the first of the occasional women that claimed their dues for killing vermin.

The year 1667 saw John Penny getting paid for three hedgehogs along with Charles Snelling for two and John Hope for one, each receiving 4d. per head. In 1668 Thomas Winton was paid 10s. for killing an unspecified number of choughs. It is stated in the 1762 account books that 1d. was paid for the head of a chough and as all payments for pests have remained the same throughout, Winton must have killed 120 birds.

East Terrace, 1900s. (STEVE RICHARDSON)

West Terrace, 1900s. (STEVE RICHARDSON)

Cliff Terrace, 1900s. (STEVE RICHARDSON)

Victoria Place, 1900s. (STEVE RICHARDSON)

Westbourne Terrace, 1900s. (STEVE RICHARDSON)

West Hill, 1900s.   (STEVE RICHARDSON)

Queen Street, c.1900.   (STEVE RICHARDSON)

No. 8, Queen Street, with resident family, c.1900.   (STEVE RICHARDSON)

West Hill, 1900s.   (STEVE RICHARDSON)

In 1671 nine foxes were killed, of these Mr Arscott's boy killed seven for which he received 7s. as a reward. The following year Robert Brayne's daughter received 4d. for a hedgehog; during that year a total of 19 hedgehogs were killed, along with 48 other birds and animals. During the year 1684 John Bedford received 1s.1d. for killing four moles and destroying the molehills in the churchyard.

During the period 1686–1774 a total of 48 foxes were killed. In 1771 the number of badgers killed totalled 21. This was followed by a drop in killings during the years 1771–75 when the total number of badgers killed amounted to 25. The slaughter of other mammals and birds diminished from the year 1763.

Briefs

Door to door collections for charity are not a modern phenomenon; in 1678 they were occurring in East Budleigh. During the seventeenth and eighteenth centuries 'briefs', in the form of royal mandates, were sent to parishes up and down the country, ordering parishioners to donate money to some supposedly deserving object. According to Tait 'the brief was so common as to be almost an early equivalent of… 'This week's good cause''. Church rebuilding, redemption for captives, victims of flood, fire and other manifold causes were all to be relieved by briefs.

The first recorded brief in the East Budleigh churchwardens' account book dates from 28 November 1678 and was for the rebuilding of St Paul's Cathedral Church in London. The sum of 'one pound fower shillings and seaven pence' was collected. On 25 September 1680 a house-to-house collection was made in the parish 'for the General Redemption of Captives', raising the sum of £3.15s.6d. The following month a collection took place for:

the poor sufferers of East [Dearham] in the County of Norfolk where whose losses by fire amounted to 19443 pounds and upwards where there was five persons burnt in the fire.

A sum of £9.9s was raised by the collection.

A door-to-door collection in 1686 raised £1.9s.2d. for French Protestants in England. In 1699, however, a brief for 'the suffering by fire at Drury Lane in the parish of St Giles in the Fields' raised just 2s.7½d. and a brief for 'colleagues in America' raised 3s.7½d. in 1763, showing that not all collections were met with such generosity. In total, eight collections were made for victims of hailstorms during this decade.

Over a period of 100 years, from the first brief in 1678, the people of East Budleigh contributed to well over 500 collections. The briefs were mainly for places outside Devon. Once such briefs became common, usually totalling up to 12 per year, entries in the account books show that around 2s. was the typical sum collected.

The Office of Overseer of the Poor

The office of overseer of the poor was established by the Poor Laws Act of 1597/8 and was made compulsory by the Poor Relief Act of 1601. The Vestry appointed at least two parishioners to the unpaid office of overseer of the poor for a period of 12 months. They were to levy a poor rate and supervise its distribution amongst the poor. In 1834 most of their duties were transferred to the Board of Guardians, however, the overseers still had the duty of assessing and collecting the poor rate. Eventually the office of overseer of the poor was abolished by the Rating and Valuation Act of 1925.

During the Middle Ages each member of a parish paid a tithe of one-tenth to the church. From this tithe the rector was to set aside one-third of the total to provide for the poor, such as orphans, the elderly and the infirm. Acts of 1388 and 1391 legitimised begging and decreed that either the birth parish of the poor should support them, or the parish where they usually lived.

In 1536 the Poor Law required better-off parishioners to raise money to support the infirm and children, as a 'matter of strong moral obligation'. Some of this money was to be made available to provide employment for the 'fit' poor. In 1563 the raising of money for the poor became a legal requirement for all parishes.

Some parishes provided poorhouses to shelter the impoverished amongst them. Funds to build these houses came from the poor rate, the level of which depended on the estimated value of property in the parish. The Poor Law Act of 1601 divided the poor receiving relief into three groups: the able-bodied who were to be found work, the impotent poor who were unable to work, and those who were simply unwilling to work.

The rate collected for the poor under the Act of 1601 was to be spent in four main ways:
1. Setting those children to work whose parents were deemed unable to maintain them.
2. Setting to work all such persons married or unmarried, who had no means to maintain themselves, and no ordinary or daily trade of life to get their living by, such as the so-called able-bodied pauper.

3. A convenient stock of flax, hemp, wood, thread, iron and other wares was to be provided for the poor to work on.

4. The lame, impotent, old, blind, and others who were poor and unable to work were to be provided with the necessary relief.

The Law of Settlement of 1662 allowed the overseer of the poor to remove a 'stranger' from the parish if he had no prospect of work within 40 days, or if he did not rent property worth £10 per annum. After 40 days, the stranger was entitled to claim settlement and poor relief in his adopted parish. A temporary worker was required to obtain a certificate from his own parish guaranteeing that he would be taken back.

The Settlement Act of 1697 allowed people to settle in a new parish providing they had a certificate guaranteeing that their home parish would take them back if they became in need of poor relief. The clothing of paupers was to be embellished with a capital P followed by a letter indicating the name of their parish.

An Act of 1723 empowered single parishes to erect workhouses; small parishes could form a union with others to make such a building viable. The poor had to remain within the premises on all days except for Sundays. Vagrants were forbidden to shelter outside the workhouse and vagrant children could be apprenticed against the wishes of their parents. As for illegitimate children, they were not necessarily given settlement certificates by the parish of their birth.

An Act of 1782 allowed the appointment of independent inspectors of workhouses. Employment for the able-bodied was provided outside of the workhouse, whereas the impotent poor were confined to indoor relief inside the workhouses. Parents were allowed to keep any children under seven years of age; orphans were boarded out. Paupers of good character no longer had to wear the pauper badge.

From 1815, the overseer of the poor gave a list of pauper lunatics to the clerk of the peace, who then laid them before Quarter Sessions.

The Poor Law Amendment Act of 1834 minimalised the provision of outdoor relief and made confinement within a workhouse the central element of the new system. It encouraged administrators of workhouses to make them unpleasant places, in an effort to deter people from seeking relief. It also became mandatory for parishes to form unions, the governing body of which was known as the Board of Guardians.

In 1913 workhouses were officially retitled Poor Law Institutions. Indoor relief was increasingly confined to the impotent poor. The Local Government Act of 1929 abolished the Board of Guardians, and the term 'pauper'. Local boroughs were encouraged to convert their workhouses into infirmaries.

Entries in the account books kept by the East Budleigh overseers of the poor during the period 1696–1860 show the diverse needs of the poor. Furthermore, it is plainly evident that money was not handed out to anyone and everyone. In 1860 the following directions were given to the overseers of the poor by the Vestry:

the overseers of the poor were to inform William Pester in that the ratepayers consider he is in a position to support his granddaughter Francis Pester and request that he will do so from this time.

The following extracts have been grouped under the various needs of the poor.

Clothing

All payments for clothing referred to the mending and making of gowns for the poor of East Budleigh. An entry regarding cloth for making the compulsory badges for paupers relates that 'a yard of red cloth and making the badges and putting then on' cost 2s., 11d. and 4s. respectively.

The Attendance of the Sick

The first entry referring to the sick receiving treatment paid for by the poor rates dates from 1706: the 'physic and blood letting of some poor people' cost the ratepayer 12s. Two years later Samuel Scott received 18s. 'for surgery to the poor'.

Payments were also made to the poor themselves: in 1720 Thomas Lavis received 7s.6d. 'at three times in his weakness'. James Follitt was repaid the 3s. he paid the doctor 'for curing his son's broken bones'.

At a Vestry meeting held in March 1769 the parishioners agreed that Dr Thomas Hodge of Sidmouth should receive the sum of three guineas 'for attending the poor and applying proper physic and surgery as often as needs shall recognise'.

Prior to the dissolution of the monasteries the church nursed the sick in monastic infirmaries, but afterwards health care became secular. As population figures rose during the eighteenth century, many hospitals were built. Exeter gained its hospital in 1741, and it is probably from this particular hospital that a patient was brought home, with a payment of 4s.2d. being made to cover the costs of the journey.

It seems, however, that the poor were not always satisfied with the quality of the treatment they received. A complaint was made to the Guardians of St Thomas Union about the conduct of the Union Doctor, Dr Kendall, who had failed to attend a dying woman in Budleigh Salterton in February 1837. A letter to the Guardians of St Thomas Union also stated that many other complaints should have been made about the same doctor, but people had been intimidated by the fact that the doctor was the son-in-law of Mr Dawe, Lord Rolle's agent. I have been unable to establish whether the Guardians acted upon this complaint.

The blind were not forgotten either. A blind school had been established in Exeter and the 1851 census records that the site of the school was St David's Hill. One of those attending the school was 28-year-old Sarah Litton who had been born in Budleigh Salterton. Whether she was also classed as poor, however, could not be established.

In 1909 a former resident of Queen Street, Budleigh Salterton, died in St Thomas Union Infirmary, aged 64 and one year later two more people from Budleigh Salterton also died there. Like many surrounding parishes, Budleigh Salterton also had its share of patients in Exminster Asylum: two former residents died there c.1910.

Burial of the Dead

The burial expenses of those who had the misfortune to die destitute were covered by the parish poor rate; such cases were the responsibility of the Local Authority. Those who died as paupers were still given a befitting funeral by means of the parish bier or, during the nineteenth century, the parish hearse.

An entry in the churchwardens' account book shows that in 1680 Mrs Pitfield's 'burial in the church' resulted in the receipt of 6s.8d. Over the years various entries give details of income from other burials.

Above: *Chassis of bier found by the author hidden in undergrowth at St Peter's burial-ground, 2004. This is probably the remains of the bier that had been given to the new Church of St Peter.* (AUTHOR)

Right: *This fully restored bier can be seen at the Exmouth Branch of Palmers' Funeral Service.*
(AUTHOR, COURTESY OF PALMERS' FUNERAL SERVICE)

A charge for 'mending the beare' was paid out of the church rates in 1685. This repair seems to have been a case of make do and mend but was, unfortunately, not a stitch in time, as a new bier had to be made the following year. The lych-gate at the entrance to a churchyard usually provided a convenient place to keep the parish bier, which was often stored in the woodwork supporting the roof.

In 1694 a 'charge for a man found dead in the parish' amounted to £1.9s.10d. which seems a princely sum considering the date.

The poor were still given a wake, as we see in an entry from the late 1700s: 'funeral charges waken and candles included' amounted to £1.2s.8d., paid for by the poor rates. Another entry gives more precise details about a wake where 'ale and cake for a funeral' were provided at the cost of 1s.8d.

An entry in the Vestry minutes for 1857 gives details of a hearse, purchased by subscription for the use of the poor. A sum of £1 per annum was to be allocated from the way rate in order to rent a coach house for the hearse. By 1863, however, the parish hearse was in need of repair. The Vestry had voted that the costs of these repairs (£1.7s.8d.) should be paid out of the way rates.

By 1871 the rent of the hearse house was to be covered by an annual charge on the poor rates of £1.10s. Furthermore, the Vestry had decided that an application should be made to the Board of Guardians for payment of this charge. The following year saw the same application being made to the Board of Guardians again. It would appear that the person who had originally provided the shelter to house the hearse was no longer able to do so, as the churchwardens were to make new arrangements. The Vestry pursued sums of money from the Board of Guardians until 1876.

According to the following extract from the Vestry minutes dated 1873, the Vestry believed that the hearse had been misused:

The keeper of the hearse will not for the future let it out until he has received payment for its use and non-

Lych-gate with granite catafalque at St Peter's burial-ground, 2004. Lych-gate roof spaces were sometimes used as a place to store the parish bier. (AUTHOR)

parishioners are not to be allowed the use of it except with the consent of the churchwardens.

The next mention of the parish hearse is in 1877 when it was resolved that 5s. should be charged for its use at the funerals of paupers.

More entries referring to the misuse of the parish hearse appear in 1866. No one was allowed to use it unless they had obtained a written order from one of the churchwardens. Both of these officials were permitted to exercise their discretion as to the sum that each applicant should pay.

The final entry referring to the parish hearse dates from 1889. At a Vestry meeting it had been decided that the charge for the shelter of the hearse was to be £1.1s. It was also decided that as the hearse belonged to the parish, anyone could hire it at 5s. for a funeral; when it was used at the funeral of a pauper, the Board of Guardians was to pay 10s.

In the early part of the twentieth century, funerals were quite grand affairs and those at East Budleigh were no exception. Transportation consisted of a hearse and pair, apparently supplied by someone called Worth. The Rolle Hotel and Feathers Inn also supplied carriages and pairs, carriages drawn by a single horse and waggonettes to convey the bearers, of whom there were generally six. By 1917 motor vehicles were gradually coming into use as a means of funeral transport.

Gloves were an important part of the funeral ritual at this time, with new gloves being purchased for each funeral. Normally white cloth gloves were the fashion, these being worn by the bearers and drivers. On some occasions kid gloves were used as well.

As mentioned in Chapter 1, the churchyard at East Budleigh had to be extended owing to the increase in population at Budleigh Salterton. The Vestry minutes for 1859 refer to land being donated by Mr Rolle and Mr Daw for the purpose of enlarging the churchyard at East Budleigh. When put to a vote, the offer was accepted by a majority of 11, but not everyone was in favour of the extension. Mr Holmes and Captain Toraino proposed the following alternative:

The Vestry gratefully acknowledge the proposed gift of Mr Rolle of a piece of freehold land and also the generosity of John Daw of the gift of his life interest therein for the enlargement of the churchyard yet most respectfully suggest (that as the Parish Church at East Budleigh is at the extremity of an extensive parish there is a great inconvenience to the inhabitants of Budleigh Salterton, Kersbrook, Knowle and Dalditch in carrying their dead so far) whether Mr Rolle will not take into his kind consideration the presentation of a piece of land more in the centre of the parish and of its population than the piece of land offered by Mr Rolle. They further take the liberty of suggesting that land in the centre of the parish will be more suitable for a public cemetery.

Although by this time, Budleigh Salterton had its own chapel of ease, the interment of the dead was to remain the jurisdiction of the mother church at East Budleigh. Budleigh Salterton folk were to wait another 40 years or so before gaining the right to bury their dead locally, as the proposed amendment was not accepted.

In 1900 the Hon. Mark G. Kerr Rolle presented Budleigh Salterton with its own burial-ground, planted with yew trees. It was consecrated by the Bishop of Crediton on 17 July of that year. The lych-gate at the main entrance to the burial-ground (also given by Mark Rolle) with its granite catafalque, still provides a convenient place to hold a short service of interment.

The cross standing in the centre of the main pathway leading away from the lych-gate is 14ft high and made of Portland stone. Mounted upon a three-stepped base, it is the work of Hems & Sons of Exeter. The side of the base facing the entrance to the churchyard is inscribed with the following:

To the Glory of God and in loving memory of the blessed dead this cross was erected by the Rev. C. Price, M.A., first vicar, and Mrs. Price, to commemorate the creation of this parish, 22nd May, 1900, and was dedicated by the Right reverend Archibald, Lord Bishop of Exeter, 8th October, 1905.

Bastardy

Bastardy was of great concern to the parish. Much was done to apprehend the men who did not contribute to the upkeep of children born out of wedlock. In 1829 overseers spent three days in London looking for one Richard Davey. They were in possession of 'a warrant to apprehend him for a Base child born on the body of Mary Causley'.

Typical offences relating to bastardy and the general non-support of a family included:

Non-payment of Bastardy Arrears.
Leaving a family chargeable to the Common Fund of the... Union.
Neglecting to provide adequate clothing for children.

Payments made at East Budleigh in regards to bastardy consisted of:

A charge for Kennard's bastard [child] 3/3d.
Concerning a base child 4/-
Expenses for the delivery and tending etc. of a base child 16/-

Here we now have the term 'base child' substituted for 'bastard', a less derogatory sounding name for a child born to unmarried parents although a stigma was still attached to it.

In January 1723 a warrant addressed to the 'Constables and Tything men of East Budleigh and all Constables and Tything men of Devon', was issued for the arrest of John Ware for fathering a 'Bastard Child' by Elizabeth Hale. From information given under oath we find that Elizabeth, 'lately deceased of East Budleigh', had been delivered of a 'female Bastard Child' some eight months previously, fathered by John Ware. The constables were ordered to apprehend John Ware on sight, take him into custody and bring him before a Justice of the Peace. This instruction to the constables concluded with the following stern warning: 'and hereof fail ye not at your peril'. We do not know whether John Ware was actually found. The people of the parish, however, seemed most determined to find him, to avoid bearing the cost of keeping his child.

An entry in the overseers' accounts from 1707 relates to a payment made to 'Margaret Lavis the

whore's charges in all £1.13s.10d.'. An 'Order' for payment dated 20 January 1728 offers an insight into the situation. Martin Randell, the father 'of a Bastard male Child born on the body of Margarett Lavis Single woman Baptised and named John' was required to pay monies to the parish. The money due was to cover costs for the birth, maintenance, nourishing and bringing up the child.

In May 1769 another order of payment ordered 'the bounden' (the father) to:

pay one shilling weekly and every week until the said Bastard Child shall attain the full age of seven years (in case he shall so long live) as and for his clothing maintenance and education and at the attainment of the said age of seven years the bounden shall pay the Churchwardens and Overseers of the Poor (of East Budleigh) the sum of forty shillings for and towards the binding of the Bastard Child apprentice to the occupier or owner of some estate in East Budleigh in case the said child shall then be in such a state of health as to be a fit and proper Object to be bound an apprentice then this Obligation shall be void or also remain in forfeiture.

An endorsement at the end of the order of payment stated that if the child was 'not a fit and proper Object to be bound an apprentice,' then the father was to pay 1s. per week 'till the child is healthy to be bound'; the weekly payment would then cease and the 40s. would be paid.

Children born out of wedlock were, however, not always kept by their mothers. One child was abandoned on a doorstep in Dalditch in 1750. Those involved related an account of this under oath to Justices of the Peace in March 1751. Grace Baxter, a single woman residing in Buckerell, bore a male child out of wedlock in the parish of Broadclist on the last day of April 1750. She took the child to East Budleigh 'as she believed it to be and carried it through a court and left it at a door of a farmhouse and put a wheelbarrow and a board before it'. It was about midnight. The child was wearing a handkerchief around its head and another around its neck; a 'woollen apron was around him and a cloak next and a cheque apron next'. Grace Baxter asserted that Joseph Ware late of Broadclist was 'ye father of ye Bastard Child above'. Richard Payton, a servant to John Thomas in a farmhouse called Dalditch, related that on 4 May 1750 at five in the morning he discovered 'something laying before the door'. It was the child 'with a board and wheelbarrow before it'. He told his master of the discovery who then sent his wife to inform the parish officers.

Elizabeth Warren of East Budleigh said the wife of John Thomas came to her between five and six in the morning and told her that a child had been found. She then went to Dalditch to see the child for herself and found him to be a boy. She kept him in her custody until she delivered him to Elizabeth Searle, about two hours later. Elizabeth Searle kept the child for four days before delivering him to Elizabeth Farrant who said she had 'had the child ever since'. She had the child baptised in the name of Richard May (the month he came to her) at East Budleigh in 1751. As for Grace Baxter, she does not explain in her oath why she chose to leave her baby in Dalditch, some 12 miles away as the crow flies from Buckerell.

In order to formally accuse a man of getting a woman pregnant out of wedlock, an 'order of bastardy' was completed. This pre-printed form had spaces for dates, names and places. One such order, dated 28 December 1805, names Sarah Stone, a single woman of East Budleigh, who was making her oath to Lord Rolle, a Justice of the Peace. The order continues:

This Examinant on her Oath, doth declare, that she is with Child, and that the said Child is likely to be born a Bastard, and to be chargeable to the said Parish of East Budleigh and the said Sarah Stone doth charge one William Pile of the said Parish of East Budleigh with having gotten the said Child on her Body, with which she is now pregnant, he the said William Pile having had carnal Knowledge of her Body on or about the month of August last and that no other Person hath had carnal Knowledge of her Body, with respect to such Child but the said William Pile and that he is the true Father of the said Child, with which she is now pregnant as aforesaid.

The order of bastardy was then signed by Sarah Stone and Lord Rolle. Strangely, Stone's hand is the better.

A total of 40 'orders of bastardy' for East Budleigh are held at the Devon Record Office, covering the period 1707–1832. By 1832 monies due from certain 'orders of bastardy' were not forthcoming and the outstanding debts of certain men were rising to mountainous proportions. A total of 15 men owed money, two of whom were in debt to the tune of nearly £32 each. As the names of these men crop up time and time again it is probably fair to presume that they rarely supported their children.

Workhouses and Almshouses

There are no references to the workhouse in the account books although the 1851 census shows one person whose birthplace was recorded as East Budleigh residing in the workhouse at Exeter. Elizabeth Arnold, a 72-year-old pauper who gave servant as her occupa-

tion, was doubtless in the workhouse as one of the 'impotent poor'. Where she lived prior to going into the workhouse is unknown and as the 1851 census makes no mention of an Arnold family in East Budleigh, it would seem she was living elsewhere.

The workhouse was a place where discipline was strict; breaking the rules could result in criminal charges and severe punishment. Those who refused to work were sentenced to seven days' hard labour by the magistrate. Clothes were deemed the property of the workhouse and dirtying them resulted in 14 days' hard labour. The use of 'obscene language to the Master of the Union House' cost the individual concerned a 5s. fine or seven days' hard labour in lieu of non-payment.

After the Second World War many workhouses passed into the hands of the National Health Service but even this did not remove the stigma attached to them. Many elderly people requiring hospitalisation still thought of the buildings as workhouses and did not wish to be placed in them.

Religious bodies and private individuals established almshouses (also called bede houses). In many cases the private benefactor stipulated the conditions under which the poor could be admitted to the house under their bequest. Mary Ash, aged 70, a former lacemaker who had been born in Knowle, probably considered herself fortunate to reside in an almshouse in St Mary Major, Exeter. The 1851 census gives her place of residence as 'No 4 Ten Cells', a small room within the almshouse and not as it sounds, in a prison.

Apprenticeships

Apprenticeship systems date from the Middle Ages when guilds of craftsmen first used contracts or indentures to govern the circumstances under which an apprentice learnt his trade. A statute of 1563 gave magistrates the power to ensure that the indentures made between masters and apprentices were adhered to. The conditions binding an apprentice to his master were written twice on one piece of paper that was then cut in two by means of a wavy line that resulted in indentations. One half was given to each party. The indents in both copies of the indentures fitted together perfectly, proving that the contract had been made between the two people concerned.

Children of poor parents were often placed into apprenticeship. During the years 1728–1832, over 100 apprentice indentures are recorded for East Budleigh. The following summarization from an indenture dated 1763 gives an insight into the conditions set for a typical parish apprentice and her mistress.

Dedication of the war memorial with additional inscriptions of those who gave their lives in the Second World War, c.1950. The photograph includes: *Mr Palmer (second from left), Mrs Southcott, Mr and Mrs Dale, Mrs Yates, Mrs Burch and Mrs Miller.* (KATH GOODING)

Above: *VE Day celebrations behind the Public Hall. Among those celebrating are Harry Sedgemore, Stan Burgess, George Mears, Len Curtis, Vera Curtis and Harold Curtis.* (NICK LOMAN COLLECTION)

Left: *Street party to celebrate the end of the Second World War. The photograph includes: Mrs Veale, Daisy Carnell and Mary Clarke.* (NICK LOMAN COLLECTION)

With the consent of His Majesty's Justices of the Peace, the parish churchwarden and an overseer of the poor would place a poor child as an apprentice to the occupier of an estate. Here the child would dwell and serve the occupier of the estate until she had accomplished her full age of 21 years or married. During this term the apprentice was required to serve her mistress faithfully in all lawful business according to her 'Power, Wit and Ability; and honestly, orderly and obediently, in all Things demean and behave herself'. The mistress was to teach good housewifery and provide 'competent and sufficient Meat, Drink and Apparel, Lodging, Washing and all other Things necessary and fit' for an apprentice. The mistress was required to provide for her apprentice to prevent her from becoming a charge to the parish and parishioners.

At the end of the apprentice's term, some estate occupiers were to 'provide, allow and deliver unto the said Apprentice double Apparel of all sorts, a good new suit for Holy-Days, and another for the Working-Days'.

Apprentices may have been well provided for, but they worked very hard. It can only be hoped that they experienced a better quality of life with their master or mistress than with their poor parents.

The overseers' account books do not include many entries referring to apprentices; examples include paying 2s. for an apprentice's indenture in 1696 and £1 for the clothing of another apprentice in 1698.

Trewman's *Exeter Flying Post* dated 21 January 1813 reported that on Sunday 10 January, Charles Weeks, an apprentice, had run away from his master, Joseph Humphry, a blacksmith of Budleigh Salterton. Weeks was 16 years old, and described as being about 5ft 1in. or 5ft 2in. tall, of slight build, with short light hair, dark eyes and a fresh countenance. He was wearing a red-and-yellow striped handkerchief about his neck and a short brown double-breasted coat, with buttons covered in the same material. He was also wearing a white cloth waistcoat with white-plated buttons and velverteen breeches and blue-and-white striped cotton stockings. A stark warning was given to 'whoever harbours or employs the said apprentice' that they would be 'prosecuted according to law'.

Settlement and Removal

If the churchwardens and overseers of the poor regarded someone as having been erroneously charged to a parish, they applied for a removal order from two Justices of the Peace. It had to be shown that the person resided in a parish without having gained settlement there, was unable to produce any certificate showing him to be settled elsewhere, and that the person had become chargeable to the parish. The Justices of the Peace would then examine the person upon oath and direct which parish was his or her lawful settlement.

In part, an order of removal ran along the following lines:

We do therefore require you the said Churchwardens and Overseers of the poor of the said parish of y, or some or one of you, to convey the said x from and out of the said parish of y to the said parish of z, and him deliver to the Churchwardens and Overseers of the poor there to some or one of them together with this our Order, or a true Copy thereof, at the same time showing to them the original, and we do hereby require you the said Churchwardens and Overseers of the said parish of z to receive and provide for him as an inhabitant of your parish.

The Devon Record Office contains numerous settlement examinations from the parish of East Budleigh, 200 of which date from the period 1673–1847. There are also over 150 removal orders for the period 1701–1856, but doubtless more actually took place. The following settlement examinations from the nineteenth century all relate to Budleigh Salterton. Whether these people were ultimately removed is not always known.

Examined in 1828, Mary Dorcey stated that she was a 57-year-old spinster born on board HMS Albion in 1771. Her father, an Irish marine, and her mother, who was from Hatherleigh, married in Plymouth. At the age of three she was placed in the care of her grandmother in Hatherleigh following the death of her mother. She was in service with Mrs O'Connor in Salterton.

In 1839, Sarah Bowden declared herself to be a spinster residing in Tiverton, the place of her birth. She was in service in Tiverton and Ilfracombe, and with Miss Manning of Salterton. The 1851 census shows Sarah living at the age of 72 as a lodger on parish relief in Tiverton.

In 1851, Tryphena Estop stated she had been born in Ottery St Mary 30 years previously. Her husband, John Estop, a dragoon, died 15 months after they had married in Exeter. After working as a yearly servant in Lympstone, Littleham, Salterton and finally Sidmouth, she was now 65 and chargeable to the parish.

When examined two years later, in 1853, Harriet Heath stated that she was a spinster, residing in Salterton. She was under an order for removal from

East Budleigh to Exeter but this was suspended due to a doctor's certificate declaring her to be suffering from chronic inflammation of the liver and having a tendency to dropsy. Although the doctor had certified her as unfit to be moved, the removal order was subsequently enforced.

The overseers' accounts also give some indication of the distances involved in certain resettlement cases. We are, for example, informed that the 'expenses for removing William Lawrence to his settlement in the parish of Bermondsey London' resulted in a cost of £5.10s.

The Criminal Poor

The account books of the overseers of the poor contain the following rather striking entry:

there was a Parish Meeting yesterday called in the Church for the parishioners, and payers to the poor met this day to consider what course to take provided any person should be guilty of any misdemeanour or felony for cutting of any person's hedges copses or woods for Brooms Stakes spars or any other use whatsoever and carry the same sticks off from the premises or for taking and carrying away of any other wood from any person's ground copse or woods or for stealing of geese ducks [corn] peas chickens apples turnips furze or turf or any other thing whatsoever.

And it was agreed on by all the payers to the poor then present that whosoever should be guilty of any misdemeanour or felony in this parish after this notice given on this day that shall be a sufferer by any of the above articles he or she being a sufferer shall desire the overseers on a Sunday to call a Parish Meeting for one day in the same week and at said meeting the aggrieved person or persons are there to lye his or their case before the payers to the poor then present And if they shall think it necessary and give the said person or persons so aggrieved direction to prosecute the said offender or offenders that then the undersigned do hereby agree that all such reasonable and necessary charges shall be repaid by overseers then being out of the poor [book] to the said prosecutor or prosecutors and we do hereby desire that this may be made a standing rule at all times hereafter until the payers to the poor shall think proper to alter it and for that purpose it is here inserted in the parish book accordingly as witness our hands in the Parish of East Budleigh the 14th day of December 1761
[Signed] J Duke.

Whether or not the account book entry indicates an epidemic of crime during this period is not clear. Was it really a case of criminals committing offences,

or were the poor and needy merely trying to provide for their families?

If the above declaration was the result of offences being committed in the parish of East Budleigh, the offenders would have been dealt with in accordance with the Vagrancy Acts. The draconian nature of these Acts becomes especially apparent when viewing records of the harsh sentences handed out to those sent to the Devon County Prison at Exeter during the second half of the nineteenth century, where stone breaking and the treadmill was part of the daily routine. Although the following are general offences for Devon as a whole they are indicative of activities recorded in the East Budleigh Vestry declaration:

Stealing eggs the value of 2 pence, 1 month's hard labour.
Stealing bread and meat, 14 days' hard labour.
Killing 3 turkeys, 4 months' hard labour [9-year-old boy].
Stealing apples (growing), pay eight shilling fine or serve 7 days' hard labour [2 boys aged 9 and 1 boy aged 11].
Stealing a rabbit and ten young, 1 month's hard labour and 3 years' Reformatory [boy aged 13].
Stealing turnips (growing), 14 days' hard labour.

At least once in prison the offenders no longer had to worry about where their next meal was coming from or where to find a bed for the night. Upon arrival they had the luxury of a bath and were seen by a medical officer. They were also provided with clothing.

Discipline was strict and the consequences of not adhering to the prison rules were severe. The Governor punished dissenting prisoners with the bread-and-water diet, the treadmill or the birch. In 1899, inmates were given bread and gruel for breakfast and supper; lunch consisted of bread with a rotation of suet pudding, potatoes and porridge. At the discretion of the medical officer, juveniles were entitled to one pint of milk per day.

The 1851 census lists the following men among those incarcerated in the Devon County Prison, Exeter: John Bourn, a gardener journeyman; William Sedgemore, fisherman; William Osborne, mariner. All three men gave their birthplace as 'Budleigh'. Prior to the imprisonment of these men, the East Budleigh overseers of the poor paid costs of 7s. in 1783 for 'the conveyance of a person to the Bridewell', i.e. the county gaol at Exeter.

A 'Funeral Furnishing' account book amongst the records of the local funeral director at Budleigh

Left: *Kersbrook Farm at the bottom of Copps Hill, c.1950. The following is written on the back of this postcard: 'you have heard of Copps Hill where the cars are tested in this part of the world – well – this farm is at the bottom of the hill… the road is very stony where they drive the cars'.*

(Nick Loman Collection)

Below: *The duty 'AA Man', splendid in his uniform, welcoming the motorist to Budleigh Salterton, c.1950.*
(Steve Richardson)

Gran and Grandad Gooding with Frank Gooding, outside the Old Cottage beside the Dog and Donkey, c.1920. Sadly, Frank died at the age of six. (Kath Gooding)

A motor bike and its admirers, c.1930. From left to right, behind: *Tim Hexter, Leonard Lee, Sid Matthews, Les Burch, Gladys Burch, Ern Heard, Jim Harris, Percy Burch;* sitting on the motor bike: *Ted Gooding, Eddy Burch, Leslie Pratt, Sam Burch.* (KATH GOODING)

Salterton records the death of a two-year-old boy in HM Prison, Exeter, in 1909. The fact that this sad event is recorded by a funeral director in Budleigh Salterton implies that the boy's mother, who would have been awaiting trial or serving a sentence in the prison, was also from the town. Sadly, the boy's coffin, with 3yds of frilling, 4yds of lining, 3lbs of flock and a satin pillow, was probably the most luxurious thing he had ever lain in.

Finally we turn to two minor criminals, named Hart and Prince, in the employ of Mr Bastion of Budleigh Salterton. They found themselves before the magistrates at Exmouth Petty Sessions in January 1856 due to a complaint from none other than Lady Rolle. The two lads were fined 19s. and 20s. respectively for leaving their wagons unattended (and presumably the horses) outside Lympany's beerhouse on the Budleigh Salterton road.

Vagrants

Throughout history, monarchs have attempted to deter vagrants. In 1495 Henry VII ordered for vagabonds to be kept in the stocks for 'three days and nights on bread and water'. In 1531 Henry VIII pronounced that an able-bodied vagrant should be 'tied to the end of a cart naked and be beaten with whips till his body be bloody'. Worse was to come in the form of the removal of an ear and eventual hanging if the vagrant persisted in his following. In 1597 transportation to America came into being, but after 1776 convicts were transported to New South Wales; branding on the shoulder with the letter 'R' for rogue occurred from 1604. Once Charles II was restored to the throne in 1660, the poor began to receive help from their parish and vagrants were treated with slightly more tolerance than had previously been the case.

The following offences under the vagrancy laws and the corresponding sentences handed out by magistrates, illustrate the hardship endured by the poor and homeless during the nineteenth century:

Begging alms, 7 days' hard labour.
Lodging in an unoccupied building without having any visible means of subsistence, 7 days' hard labour.
Wandering abroad and lodging in the open air, not having any visible means of subsistence, 7 days' hard labour.
Endeavouring to obtain and gather alms by exposing wounds.
Hawking without a licence.
Wandering abroad and lodging in an outhouse not having any visible means of subsistence and not giving a good account of himself for which he subjected himself to be dealt with as a Rouge and Vagabond, 3 months' imprisonment.

Budleigh Salterton had its own 'rogue and vagabond' in the form of Anna Maria Reed. The following order is addressed to:

the Keeper of the House of Correction... and also all Constables and other Officers of Peace whom it may concern to receive and convey, and to the Churchwardens or Overseers of the Poor of East Budleigh to receive and obey.

In the order it is stated that:

Whereas Anna Maria Reed on the 2ⁿᵈ day of May 1817 was apprehended in the Parish of St Thomas the Apostle wandering in an Idle and Disorderly manner – a reputed thief after having been sent to her parish by a Vagrants Pass And whereas the said Anna hath been by me a Justice of the Peace examined adjudged and convicted to be a Rogue and Vagabond and hath in consequence of the conviction been committed to and confined in the House of Correction... for the space of seven days.

Anna's last legal settlement was found to be in the parish of East Budleigh. This meant that at the end of her seven days of imprisonment she was to be conveyed to East Budleigh and 'delivered to some Churchwarden or Overseer of the Poor' who was required to 'receive and provide for her'.

Anna did not, however, return to East Budleigh upon completion of her prison sentence, but made her way back to Exeter. Once again she was apprehended as a 'Rogue and Vagabond' and convicted of having 'committed an Act of Vagrancy' for which she received a further seven days' imprisonment. Her prison record shows that she was 19 years old, of short stature with a fresh complexion and dark-brown hair. Again her last legal settlement was given as the parish of East Budleigh where she had been born.

The constables of Exeter were given the following instructions:

Convey the said Vagrant to the Parish of St Thomas the Apostle (that being the first Precinct or the next Precinct through which she ought to pass in the direct Way to the Parish of Budleigh Salterton to which she is to be sent) and deliver her to the Constables or other Officers of St Thomas with this pass taking his receipt for the same And the said Vagabond is there to be conveyed on to the Parish of Budleigh Salterton there to be delivered to some Churchwarden or Overseer of the Poor of the same Parish and they are required to receive her and provide for her the said Vagrant. Dated 21 November 1817.

The order directing the conveyance of Anna, 'vagrant and reputed thief', to Budleigh Salterton is very detailed; she was treated as a piece of baggage, not as a human being.

An entry containing a direct reference to vagrancy in the overseers' accounts appears in 1832 when 'Perriam's bill for food for a vagrant confined at the Inn Salterton' amounted to 9s.9s.

A case of begging was brought to the attention of Budleigh Salterton people in the latter part of 1893. A man had been begging in Budleigh Salterton with a book purporting to contain the vicar's 'recommendation of the case' and with the vicar's name 'down for a subscription' (thus implying that the vicar himself had made a payment). The vicar made it known to the parishioners that he 'never, under any circumstances, writes a 'brief' or commendatory notice, or appeal for subscriptions, for anyone'. The vicar further stated that 'any applicant professing to beg under his sanction is an impostor'. He then told his parishioners that should a similar situation occur in the future, they should inform both the police and himself, and retain the book or 'brief' in question.

Miscellaneous Payments
The following entries in the account books of churchwardens and overseers of the poor offer insight into various aspects of the lives of our ancestors. The entries date from 1691 to 1835:

Paid Elizabeth Hill for candle burnt when the French were on the coast 1/6d.
Payments made by churchwardens and overseers of the poor Paid unto Henry Leat for several journeys to Exeter [due to false accusations made] by John Bending and his charge in bringing him the said Bending to account £1.
Also this account [charges] for horse hire for several journeys to Exeter in taking out the moneys and other charges about the said John Bending to his account with Henry Leat in the year 1698 £1/10/-
Wood for the poor 9/3d.
Those that cannot nor are able to pay [their rates] and will not 14/9d.
Seven bushels of malt for Agnes Nuberry at £1/1/-
Teaching the [Dame] boy to mend shoes 8d.
Half a year's Land tax want [i.e. minus] 8d due from John Satchel at Salterton and he 'being turned out craves the liberty of the said money to be paid by the Overseers' £2/19/4d.
Expenses on Budley fair day for ale 1/6d.
The use of a donkey to go to Woodbury 1/-
Expenses for beer and cake at the settling accounts 3/4d.
Paid for coming from Salterton to give information at

the inn in childbirth 9d.
Paid for assistance in trying the weights and measures 2/-
Paid for drawing lime and drawing J Lugg to Sidmouth 4/3d.

Payments were also made for 'Pound Tax'. This relates to the parish enclosure used to confine stray animals for which the owner had to pay a fine to retrieve them. From 1815, lists of pauper lunatics were sent to the Clerk of the Peace. 'Drawing up a list of lunatics' by the overseers at East Budleigh cost 6d.

Benefactors

Benefactors gave aid to the poor through money and gifts. As an example of this a deed of gift dated 3 April 1638 records Phillip Wotton as donating 5s. a year to the 'poor of East Budleigh forever'. This money was to be paid to the poor at 'Christide out of his lands in Salterton'. In furtherance of this gift he bequeathed the following:

afterward by his last will and testament bearing date ye twenty-sixth of October 1657, hee gave six shillings and eight pence yearly to the poor of this parish forever to bee paid out of the same lands and at the same time aforesaid.

In 1793 the overseers' account book records that Gilbert Cowd had delivered 'a silver watch to have it righted for the parish in order to make the best of it'. To what use the overseers made of this benefactor's gift, if indeed a use was made of it, is not known. Lord and Lady Rolle also made donations to the poor. On one occasion in January 1842 they distributed 'nine fine bullocks among the poor of various parishes including Budleigh'.

Subscriptions

The minutes of a Vestry meeting in September 1853 indicate that all was not well between the representatives of the so-called 'land side' of the parish and the 'town side'. The purpose of the Vestry meeting was the formation of a committee to raise a subscription in aid of the poor. It seems that the poor in the 'town side' were struggling with the high prices of provisions there. The minutes state that no parishioner from the land side attended, yet they must have been aware of the impending meeting – a notice of it would have been posted, as always, on the church door. Nevertheless, the town side continued with the meeting in the absence of representation from the land side. It was agreed, perhaps unsurprisingly, that a subscription should commence for the purpose of providing relief to the poor of the town side. Nothing further appears about this incident.

Also funded by subscription was a soup kitchen during the severe weather of 1895. The kitchen opened on 15 February for a four-week period. During this time, 600 quarts of soup and 432 loaves of bread were consumed.

The Office of Constable

The office of constable derives from the term 'comes stabuli' (count of the stables), an early medieval office of state that is probably the oldest of all parochial positions. Nominated at Vestry meetings held at the end of February and the beginning of March, constables were almost wholly responsible for the maintenance of law and order within the parish. They sometimes affixed the staff of office, a sign of authority, to the outside door of their house. Constables had powers of arrest that were frequently exercised; they could take into custody anyone who had committed a felony or who was committing a breach of the peace. Those arrested could be placed in the stocks, the roundhouse (place of detention), the Cage (a temporary lock-up in the village), or even the constable's own house until it was possible to bring them before a magistrate. The wide range of duties performed by the constable included the following:

The supervision of Watch and Ward as specified by the Statute of Winchester, 1285.
The upkeep of the stocks, lock-up and other means of punishment and imprisonment.
The inspection of alehouses and the suppression of gaming houses.
The apprenticing of pauper children.
The supervision and removal, where necessary, of itinerant strangers and beggars.
Collaboration with other officials in the relief of the poor.
The collection of the county rate and of any specially levied national tax.
The maintenance of the parish arms and the training of the local militia.
The convening of parish meetings.
The care of the parish bull.
The presentation of parishioners who did not attend church regularly.
Assistance at shipwrecks in the locality.
The apprehension and detention of suspected criminals, the arrest of escaped prisoners.
The suppression of riots and unlawful assemblies.
The compilation of jurors' lists.
The collection of child maintenance from fathers of illegitimate children.

W.G. Harding's general store and Post Office at Knowle, 1920s. (STEVE RICHARDSON)

Knowle Village, 1920s. The man in the uniform is Arthur Gooding. Above the thatched cottage on the right is the Harris's house. On the left-hand side of the road are the houses of the Farr, Bowles and Hillman families. (KATH GOODING)

The Britannia, Knowle, 1900s. The wagon has the date 1905 and belongs to Tozer's, builders from Ottery. The sign above the doorway names W. Bastin as a licensed retailer of beer, cyder, tobacco, etc., 'to be consumed on the premises'. (STEVE RICHARDSON)

The Britannia, 1910, but on this occasion it is not possible to read the sign above the door. At this time the Britannia was situated in front of the present Britannia Inn, or 'Dog and Donkey', as it was known. (STEVE RICHARDSON)

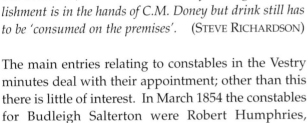

The Britannia, c.1910. At the time of writing the establishment is in the hands of C.M. Doney but drink still has to be 'consumed on the premises'. (STEVE RICHARDSON)

Children posing for the camera at Knowle, c.1900.
(KATH GOODING)

The main entries relating to constables in the Vestry minutes deal with their appointment; other than this there is little of interest. In March 1854 the constables for Budleigh Salterton were Robert Humphries, Walter Kerslake and Pitman Halsey.

At a Vestry meeting held during December 1854 it was agreed that the parish required two policemen. A committee was appointed to establish the necessary costs involved and also to enquire about the levying of a rate. In January 1855, however, a total of nine inspectors of police were appointed within the parish: four for the land side, four for the town side and one for Knowle.

Following on from the appointment of the nine inspectors of police, the Vestry discussed the appointment of two constables to be funded through the levying of a rate. At this time, the general public was slowly beginning to accept the presence of a permanent police force. The Metropolitan Police Act of 1829 had allowed for a police force in London, whilst the County Police Act of 1839, albeit not mandatory, allowed for police forces elsewhere in the country.

We learn no more of paid constables until January 1856 when the Vestry proposed to levy a police rate of £100. Two parishioners found the prospect of a police rate contentious and proposed that it should not be allowed. A show of hands revealed that 40 of the ratepayers were in favour of the rate, whilst 37 were against it. There were calls for a poll of the entire parish, but whether this took place is not recorded.

In 1855 the inspectors of police requested that the February Vestry meeting of 1856 be delayed, as the parish police rate had only been partially collected. This would imply that certain parishioners were holding back their contributions to the rate, possible because they did not agree with it.

Harry Cummings, postman at Knowle, 1924.
(KATH GOODING)

When the Vestry meeting eventually took place, on Saturday 14 February, the chairman, inspectors and treasurer resigned their offices. Why? Quite simply the police had been taken over by the chief constable of the county and a county police force was in the making. The 1856 County and Borough Police Act had established police forces in the areas of the country which had not already done so.

The constables appointed by the Vestry in 1858 were as follows: Samuel Connett, blacksmith; Walter Kerslake, baker; William Pile, farmer; Robert [Finch?], mason; James Webber junr, cordwainer (shoemaker); Samuel Austin, mason; George Perriman, grocer; William [Widgery?], baker. The scope of their duties at this time was probably to assist the other parish officers.

At the Devon Quarter Sessions held at the Castle of Exeter on 3 July 1866 it was ordered that the lock-up at Budleigh Salterton was to be leased for seven years at a rent of £2 per annum. A maximum sum of £1.7s. was granted to cover the necessary repair of the lock-up. The terms of the lease were referred to the Police Committee for settlement.

In 1867 the constables for the parish were as follows: Samuel Austin; William Pile; Ellis Sage; Walter Keslake; William Annis; James Webber; Joseph Park; S.H. Williams; John [Barrs?]; James Wortham; Samuel Cornett; Samuel Pile.

Street Lighting and Night Watch

'The supervision of Watch and Ward as specified by the Statute of Winchester 1285' tops the list of a constable's duties on p.69. 'Watch' referred to the need for townships to 'arrange guards at night and apprehend suspicious persons'. 'Ward' referred to daytime duties. The modern-day neighbourhood watch scheme shares the principles of 'Watch and Ward'. Incidentally, the term 'Hue and Cry' also stems from the Statue of 1285, whereby a person wishing to make an arrest could call on other parishioners to assist him. Even today, a police constable can call on a member of the public to assist him or her in making an arrest.

In order to support the night watch, Local Acts of 1750 permitted the levying of a rate to pay for street lighting, whilst the Lighting and Watching Act of 1833 allowed towns with a population of over 5,000 to appoint paid watchmen.

It was not until January 1855 however, that the Vestry at East Budleigh made any effort to have street lighting. Whether to adopt the 1833 Act of George IV in regards to 'lighting and watching of parishes' had been debated, but nothing came of the discussion. However, a meeting in August 1867 was to result in a positive outcome for Budleigh Salterton. The Churchwardens of East Budleigh gave notice that:

having received an application from four ratepayers of the said Parish requesting that we will appoint and notify pursuant to the Stutures 3 & 4 Wm 4 & 90 Sec 5 a time and place for a public meeting of the ratepayers of the said Parish for the purpose of determining whether so much of the Provisions as relate to lighting contained in a certain Act made and passed in the 4th year of the reign of his late Majesty King George the Fourth for the lighting and watching of parishes in England and Wales and to make provisions in lieu thereof be adopted and carried into execution in the said parish We do appoint a public meeting of the ratepayers of the said parish to be held at the Vestry Room on Monday 5th day of August 1867 at 11 o'clock in the forenoon for the purpose of determining whether so much of the provisions as relate to lighting in the said Act shall be adopted and carried into execution in the said Parish. Dated the 27th day of July 1867.
[Signed] Fred Blandy and John Cockeram, Churchwardens.

At the meeting of 5 August 1867, a motion to adopt lighting was lost as there was an insufficient number of ratepayers in attendance. Those who had requested the meeting were Thomas Trickey, Walter Keslake, Samuel Strickland and John Harwood, they being persons paying rates for the relief of the poor of the parish and also residing within the part of the parish to have street lighting.

Captain Charles Torriano was appointed chairman of another meeting that was held at 11 o'clock on Monday 19 August at the Rolle Arms Hotel, Budleigh Salterton. The purpose of this meeting was to determine whether lighting should be 'adopted and carried into execution' under the 1833 Street Lighting and Night Watch Act in the following parts of the parish:

Budleigh Salterton, Little Knowle, Granary and Stoneborough extending from the top of Salterton Hill to the Lime Kiln, and surrounded or Comprised by or within the following roads, streets and ways that is to say the beach at Budleigh Salterton, Lime Kiln Lane, Stoneborough Lane, Greenaway Lane, Hall's Lane, Hall's Hill and the Common at the top of Salterton Hill before mentioned and thence straight to the Cliff and including in the said part of the said parish all and every the Messuages or Tenements and Homesteads with the Appurtences situate out of the aforesaid limits but adjoining or contiguous to any of the aforesaid part of the said Roads Streets and Ways.

A vote indicated that only five people were against lighting the district, whilst 38 people were in favour. Seven ratepayers were to act as inspectors, and were also to collect a sum not exceeding £110 from the ratepayers during the ensuing year .

Not long after the adoption of the Lighting Act, the streets of Budleigh Salterton were illuminated by gas lamps. The evening of Wednesday 11 December

Little Knowle, 1900s. (STEVE RICHARDSON)

Above: *Little Knowle, c.1906.* (STEVE RICHARDSON)

Left: *Little Knowle, c.1900s.* (STEVE RICHARDSON)

1867 was set for the grand occasion when the lighting would come into effect for the first time.

During the period of time which elapsed between the adoption of the Lighting Act and the resulting illumination of the streets, the Budleigh Salterton Gas Company was formed. Those undertaking to form a gas company had interviewed engineers and contractors on various occasions, but without positive results. Seemingly by chance, Messrs Stears, Brothers & Company of Hull, chose Budleigh Salterton as a holiday destination. During their visit they proposed terms for the formation of a company and made more attractive proposals for the building of the requisite works than had previously been tendered. A total of 600 shares were raised at £5 per share to start the company, of which the Hon. Mark Rolle became patron as well as a shareholder. Mr W. Strickland of Budleigh Salterton carried out the building of the gasworks which were erected near the junction of Stoneborough Lane with Granary Lane. As there was no Board of Local Health at Budleigh Salterton, notices had to be given and a public meeting held with respect to the erection of the public lamps. A rate of 6d. in the pound was levied, and this enabled the company to erect 30 public lamps for which the tariff charged was £2.18s. per annum for each.

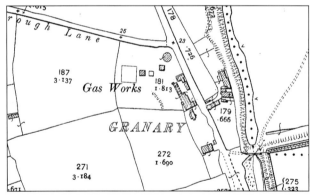

The 1934 Ordnance Survey map of the gasworks (scale: 25in to 1 mile; reduced). (CLINTON DEVON ESTATES)

As a spin-off some of Budleigh Salterton's inhabitants had the gas installed in their private houses and places of business. Nearly 100 services were laid from the main into private establishments, whilst it was hoped that another 150 services would be taken up before the winter was out. The gas was charged at 6s.8d. per 1,000 cu. ft, this being thought a reasonable amount as many towns much larger than Budleigh Salterton and having burnt gas for many years paid a higher rate.

Returning to the day on which the inaugural lighting of the streets was to take place, it was said of Budleigh Salterton that:

throughout the day this pretty little seaside town was in one joyous commotion. Decorations were visible in almost every direction; and a large number of visitors from the neighbouring places imparted an unusual briskness to this charming watering-place, famous as it is for its pebbly beach and its other distinct attractions.

The Hon. Mark Rolle had been invited to take the chair at the public dinner but was unable to attend due to a previous engagement. Lady Rolle had been requested to formally light the first lamp, but was likewise unable to be present. She had, however, informed the committee that 'if she had been at home it would have given her great pleasure to have acceded to their wish'. As a consequence of the Rolles being absent, Mr R. Lipscombe, the steward of the Rolle Estate, was invited to preside at the dinner, and Mrs Lipscombe was asked to light the first lamp. They both accepted.

About 120 people attended the dinner held at the Public Rooms and were entertained by the Exmouth Volunteer Artillery Band. Just prior to six o'clock, the band lead the way from the Public Rooms to the Post Office where the ceremony of lighting the gas burners was to take place. The Exmouth Volunteer Artillery Band led a procession of the decoration committee around the town, the directors and inspectors bearing torches with four torchbearers mounted on grey horses bringing up the rear. The final device was lit at the Public Rooms, after which the illumination was complete. It was reported that 'the effect of the artificial lights throughout gave to Budleigh Salterton an exceedingly pretty appearance'.

A ball held at the Public Rooms, attended by more than 100 people, brought the evening's festive proceedings to a close. The following evening a tea was provided for 130 of the working-class folk of Budleigh Salterton. This tea was funded by the wealthier inhabitants of the town, who also provided entertainment.

The Office of Waywarden

The Highway Act of 1555 established the office of waywarden, also known as surveyor of the highway. The waywarden was unpaid and appointed by the parishioners. After 1691 justices appointed the waywarden at their special 'Highway Sessions' from a list of holders of land supplied by the parish. Three times a year the waywarden had to view and report upon road conditions to the justices. He was responsible for appointing the days for statute labour – abolished by an Act of 1835 – when fellow parishioners were supervised in the odious task of repairing the roads. If the elected person chose not to perform this compulsory office, a monetary penalty was incurred. After the office of constable, this was perhaps the least popular in the parish.

Development of Roads

Writing in the sixteenth century, Risdon described travelling in Devon as 'rough and unpleasant to strangers' as the ways were 'cumbersome and uneven', even describing them as 'painful for man and horse'. Vancouver, writing in 1808, says that 'particularly through the red loam district' the roads 'are very indifferent; nay, bad indeed'.

Devon roads followed early trackways and carried traffic of packhorses with their diverse loads until the early-nineteenth century when they were superseded by carts and wagons. Similarly, on the arrival of the railway, the stagecoach network went into decline; even so, Devon lagged behind other parts of England in the development of a transport system.

Turnpike trusts set up in the eighteenth century cut new roads and greatly improved road surfaces and gradients on principal routes; side-roads, though, were mainly left untouched. The Highway Amendment Act of 1864 gradually saw the end of the turnpike trusts.

Speed and Safety

The 'Red Flag' speed limit of 4mph declared in 1865 was raised to 14mph in 1896 and to 20mph in 1903. A year later the tarring of roads took place. The 20mph speed limit was abolished outside built-up areas in 1930.

A letter concerning speed written by Mrs J.H.F. Foster of Tidwell House, published in the Western Morning News, and dated 21 Febuary 1934 was read aloud at a meeting of the Budleigh Salterton Council. The letter drew attention to the dangerous corner between Frewins and Knowle. Mr Hooker, a council member, proclaimed it was time that the council introduced a speed limit for the road, demanding 'must people be killed before some motorists can be made to drive at a decent rate?' Another member of the council was of the opinion that speeding was responsible for 70 per cent of road accidents. It was decided that the word 'SLOW' should be painted on the roadway approaching the dangerous corner.

During the years 1918–39 about 6,000 motorists were killed on British roads each year. As a result of this, new speed limits and driving tests were introduced towards the end of this period.

The Local Road Network

Studying the minutes of Vestry meetings from the period 1851–1871, as well as the waywardens' account books for the years 1803–1833, reveals much about the roads of East Budleigh, as well as the men employed to work on them.

In 1803 waywardens collected the highway rates for East Budleigh in two portions: the town side and the land side.

By 1822 the extent of the East Budleigh parish road network was recorded as being 24 miles 47 chains* and 3 yards. Those associated with Budleigh Salterton (the figures representing miles, chains and yards respectively) were:

Little Knowle Lane to the Exmouth Common Road from Salterton 0 57 2.
Ells Moor Lane to Bedlands Lane 0 65 2.
Luckeyses Lane over Halls Brook to Salterton Hill 0 61 0.
From Salterton to Pool Head Little Lane 0 8 3.
Granary Lane to the End 0 19 0.
Vills Lane to the Lime Kiln 0 46 0.
Greenway Lane to Stoneborough 0 50 1.
Wise Lane from Salterton 0 29 2.
Cop Hill Lane to Kersbrook 0 36 0.
From Cross at Leeford through Salterton and through Kersbrook to Cross past 2 43 0.

Whilst some of the above roads gained their names from the locations they were leading to or from, others were named after people who lived there, or owned property in the vicinity. Greenway, with its name implying a grassed lane, may have been a former drove-road. The fact that it also lies in the direction of Budleigh Haven may suggest that it was once used as an access to take goods to and from the harbour.

Payment and Conditions for Road Workers

The roads were built and maintained through manual labour, a most arduous task, for which general day labourers were paid 1s.2d. per day. The cost of rocks or stones purchased by the boatload varied from 5s.6d. to 10s. This variation in price may have been due to the size of the boat or the distance involved. There is no indication as to where the boats landed in order to unload their cargoes, but the area of beach by the limekilns would have been a suitable place for the task of discharging rock or stone. The materials were then conveyed to the site by horse and cart, this was known as 'team work'. In 1836 'two carts one horse each' were remunerated at 7s. a day and one 'cart and two horses' received the sum of 5s. In this year

* 1 chain = 66ft

A day out by charabanc, 1920s. The passengers include: *Revd Edmunds, George Treherne* (to his left in line with the pole), *Harold Curtis, Len Curtis, Bob Easton, George Bennett and Charlie Mears* (with the pipe).

(Nick Loman Collection)

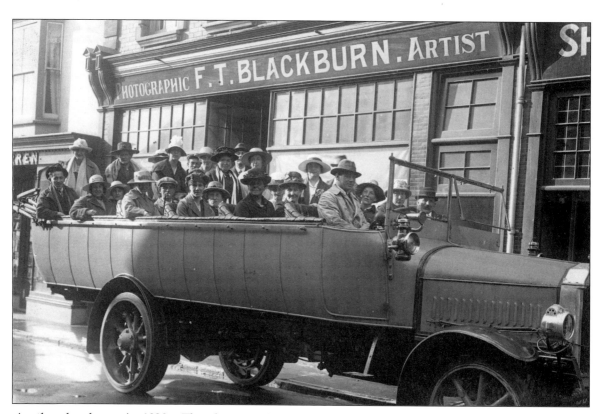

Another charabanc trip, 1920s. The photograph includes *F.T. Blackburn* (front right).

(Steve Richardson)

A visit to Chedder Caves, 1920s.

(NICK LOMAN COLLECTION)

An outing for E.W. Bastin, the builders, 1950s. Among the firm's members are: Sam Log, Bill Clemence, Herbert Till, Harry Channing, Mr Bastin, Bob Bartlett, George Gooch, ? Hinman, Ted Bentham, John Loman, Mr Humphries, Mr Chapman, Arthur Wilson, Eric Loman, Fred Trick, Charles Perry and Harry Carnell.

(NICK LOMAN COLLECTION)

17 different people with 42 carts were listed in the waywarden's account book and paid a total of £11.19s.2d.

Once the stones had been delivered to the site they had to be broken up. In 1836, John Barratt was paid 3s. for breaking 3 tons of stones; there is no mention of exactly how long the job took him. In the waywarden's accounts, there are also details of payments made in compensation for damage caused by the stone breakers, such as the sum of 3s. for broken glass, paid in 1834. Road builders were also responsible for damage to a private wall during the improvement of Kersbrook Hill. A mason was paid 17s.6d. to repair it.

During 1835 a total of 397 days of labour were worked on the roads by 15 men. In the same year Thomas Best, whose status is merely described as 'a boy', was given the sum of 1s. for gathering stones over two days. Flint and gravel for the road building were obtained by digging. Stones from the beach were also used and in 1842, 6d. was paid for them. In the same year, the cost of building 48yds of road in Dalditch amounted to 18s., which works out at 4½d. per yard. Trees and turf were used to construct hedge banks during road building or when road improvements were being fabricated, whilst timber was needed for handrails for bridges and fences. As well as the manual labour, at a cost of 1s.2d. per day, the other craftsmen required to complete walls, bridges etc., included masons, carpenters and black-smiths.

The 1834 rate included a charge imposed on 'keepers of horses and carriages'. An error rated J. Humphries for a 'waggon and two horses' when in fact he only had a 'cart and one horse'.

For the year 1844, the total costs spent on the roads for the land side were £66.16s.1d., whilst the town side costs totalled £123.7s.5d. Compared with the year 1803, rates had risen 12-fold. As in modern times, new developments were subject to vandalism. In 1839 a reward was made available 'to persons who will inform of the person or persons committing depredations to the Town Bridge'.

By 1853 Henry Leatt, a rate payer, suggested that two waywardens be appointed for the land side of the parish, being one for Salterton (where William Staddon was to take office) and one for Knowle. Each waywarden was to employ men on alternate weeks to work on the roads.

Conditions under which the road workers were employed were strictly laid down at the Vestry meeting. They were only to work on three days of the week during the period from Ladyday (25 March) to Michaelmas (29 September), and on five days of the week from Michaelmas to Ladyday. The workmen were to be paid 1s. a day for the ensuing year. A stipulation was also made that men employed as fishermen were not to be employed on the roads, and nor were any non-parishioners.

The year 1857 saw an increase in the payments for team work. A man with a cart and one horse received an increase of 6d. which meant he was paid a total of 4s. for a day's labour. A man with a cart and two horses was given an increase of 2s., bringing his wages up to 7s. per day.

In October 1857 the Vestry decided to improve the road between Tidwell and Knowle Crossing by increasing its width in places. James Prior of Otterton was to do the following:

77

*put up a new hedge across two fields in Mr Leatt's farm
called Holdstones and to plant and fence the new hedge
and to make the road twenty feet wide and take and
draw away all overplus from the road in carts as well as
draw away all turf and other material that may be want
for ten pounds.*

In May of the following year, however, the ratepayers
decided that the widening of the road between
Tidwell and Knowle Crossing was not to take place
after all. In minutes dated December 1858 the
widening of the road was once again on the agenda.
It seems that originally there had been objections to
the widening scheme, but solutions had been found.

Mr Coldridge, who was acting on the part of Mr
Rolle, stated to the Vestry that there would be no
objection to allow part or portion of Deepway Field
to be taken:

*provided that if Mr Rolle should require it the fence of
the Deepway Field should be stone ditched three feet
high and provided also that the road be not widened
more than two thirds of the length of the Deepway Field
on Mr Rolle's side.*

Mr Hine consented to any part of his land from
'Shortwood Lane towards Tidwell House being used
in the same condition', as Mr Rolle had required. Mr
Hine's tenant, Henry Leat, along with Mr Rolle's, had
also consented to the preconditions for the widening
of the road.

Mr Rolle and Mr Hine were thanked and their
offers accepted on their terms. The road from Short
Woods Cross to Madam's Landyway was to be
widened to 17ft. Tenders were to be submitted to the
waywardens; the person offering to do the work at
the least cost was to be accepted.

In May of the following year a proposition was
put to the Vestry by Alfred Short that he would
'exchange a small piece of land at Little Knowle' to
enable the road there to be 'straightened and a turn in
the road made safe and commodious'. The Vestry
minutes give no details as to the land which was to be
exchanged, but it was agreed that the work should
proceed.

Road widening was under discussion again in
February 1868 after Mr Rolle consented to give up the
necessary land between Westbourne Terrace and the
Public Rooms. The road was to be widened to about
24ft, for a distance of 240ft from the corner of
Westbourne Terrace to the corner of the Public
Rooms. A dyke-fence, 2.5ft high and turfed with a
thorn and beech hedge, was to be constructed. Mr
French was to do the work for the sum of £18. The

costs involved in the project included the following:

*Limestone for the wall, ten pounds.
Labour, four pounds.
Railing off and making good the road, one pound.
Eight hundred thorn, at two shillings and six pence per
two hundred, one pound.
Dyke walling, two pounds.*

The ratepayers would pay £15 whilst the remaining
£3 were to be funded through donations. The
Highway Board was requested to sanction the work.

Upon becoming an urban authority in April 1879,
Budleigh Salterton was to maintain its own roads.
With the local Government Act of 1894 the mainte-
nance of highways became the responsibility of the
Rural District Councils.

Transport

Whilst traffic was not the responsibility of the
waywardens – as we have seen, they controlled the
building and maintenance of roads – this nonetheless
seems an appropriate place to look at the horse-
drawn transport in and around Budleigh Salterton.

The packhorse was one of the earliest means of
transporting goods and merchandise around the
poor-quality roads of Devon. Towards the end of
the eighteenth century, carriers' carts replaced packhorses, providing horse-drawn conveyance for those
travelling to Exeter from Budleigh Salterton.
Coaches became the predominant means of travel in
the early-nineteenth century.

Trewman's *Exeter Flying Post* reported in June
1836 of a regular service by a 'light coach' operated
by Stephen's & Company, which left Exeter every
morning excepting Sundays at 8a.m. for Topsham,
Exmouth and Budleigh Salterton, returning the same
evening. In 1843 The Rapid left the New London Inn,
Exeter at 7.30a.m. for Exmouth, Budleigh Salterton
and Sidmouth on a Monday, Wednesday, Friday and
Sunday, whilst another coach left the Globe Inn at
Exeter for Exmouth and Budleigh Salterton at 5p.m.
Abraham Freeman & William Seward of Budleigh
Salterton owned an omnibus called The Magnet that
plied its business on the Salterton to Exeter road. The
partnership, for whatever reason, was dissolved on 9
March 1844.

From a guidebook published in 1842 it was noted
that 'sedan chairs and other hand conveyances for
invalids are kept [at Budleigh Salterton] by three
persons there'; by 1845 four people were in possession of such transportation. This guide also reveals
that access to and from Budleigh Salterton had
increased: the St David 'steam packet' from Topsham

and Exmouth to London operated once a week in the summer and once every ten days in the winter. It was also possible to travel to and from Exeter every day by coach or omnibus. White's *Directory of Devon* of 1850 reveals that the coaches stopped at the Rolle Arms in Budleigh Salterton and that James Austin, Emanuel Harding and George Tuck of Budleigh Salterton all sent carriers to Exeter on four days of the week.

A passenger service was also provided, twice-daily, by the Royal Mail in 1851, with coaches leaving the New Inn at Exeter at 5.30a.m. and 12p.m. for Exmouth and Budleigh Salterton. For the return journey to Exeter, coaches left Budleigh Salterton at 11.30a.m. and 5.30p.m. The fare to Exmouth was 2s. for inside passengers and 1s. for outside passengers. The Royal Mail placed a notice describing its service in Trewman's *Exeter Flying Post*. The notice was headed 'Exmouth and Budleigh Salterton' and contained the following information:

Her Majesty's Royal Mails leave the New Inn at Exeter for the above distinguished and fashionable watering-places every day at 5.30 a.m. and 12.15 p.m. returning at 12 o'clock noon in time for the up express train and 8 p.m. in time for the mail train to London. Fares to Exmouth and back 2 shillings.

Knowle Hill, pictured during the first decade of the twentieth century. (STEVE RICHARDSON)

The above advert indicates the existence of a further means of travel, the train, albeit from Exeter.

Of course, then as now, where there is transport, there is often the opportunity for accidents to occur. In February 1852 unbeknown to the driver, a 12-year-old girl climbed onto the back of the evening mail coach which was on its way from Budleigh Salterton to Exmouth. On attempting to get down, she became entangled in the back wheels of the coach. The driver heard her cries and reined in the horses. When the girl had been extricated, it appeared that she had broken both legs. She was taken to a nearby house and medical assistance was sought. Exact details of her 'severe' injuries are not given, although it is noted that she was getting better.

There was another mishap involving the 'Budleigh Mail' in January 1857. Mr Perry of Exmouth was making his way to Budleigh Salterton on horseback. On arriving at Knowle Hill at 6.30p.m., he met the mail coach coming from Budleigh on its journey to Exeter. Spooked by the lamps of the coach, his horse shied. Whether Mr Perry fell off his horse or suffered any injuries is not disclosed.

By 1860 there were three mails to Budleigh Salterton from Exeter each day: the first left Exeter

The junction of Exmouth Road and Knowle Hill with an Automobile Association telephone box, 1920s.

(STEVE RICHARDSON)

after the arrival of the mail train from London; the second, a four-horse mail coach, left at 10.45a.m. whilst the third left Exeter at 4p.m.

By 1897, however, Kelly's *Directory* lists only one coach as regularly travelling between the Rolle Arms Hotel, Budleigh Salterton, and Exmouth. The coach concerned was connected with the London & South Western Railway, which was represented locally by their agent George Hayne of the High Street, Budleigh Salterton.

High Street, 1900s. The building with the double doors and cart outside is where the Post Office stands in 2004.
(STEVE RICHARDSON)

High Street, 1900s. (NICK LOMAN COLLECTION)

High Street, 1900s. There was a farmyard in Queen Street at this time hence the cowpats.
(KATH GOODING)

Left and below: *The High Street in the days of the horse, 1900s.* (STEVE RICHARDSON)

The High Street from Fore Street, c.1900. Cowd's haircutting and shampooing saloon is on the right with Bennett's, the ironmongers, further along the street.

(STEVE RICHARDSON)

Above and below: *The High Street in the days of the motor car, 1930–60.* (STEVE RICHARDSON)

Bridges

Legislation in 1531 permitted the levying of a county rate for the upkeep of bridges; prior to this they had been the responsibility of parishes or landowners. During the fifteenth-century, wooden bridges in Devon were replaced by stone ones. One stone bridge built in 1310, thought to be the only one of its kind still in existence, lies not too far from Budleigh Salterton at Clyst St Mary. Doubtless this significant bridge probably goes unnoticed by drivers of cars making their way along the busy dual carriageway to Exeter or the motorway.

The churchwardens' accounts of 1600 show the levying of a rate for the building of bridges at Salterton. In 1680 the sum of 4d. was spent on 'parchment for a bridge rate'. The overseers' accounts for 1718 also show a payment of 15s.6d. for a bridge at Salterton. Whether this payment included labour charges as well as the price of the materials is not shown.

The above bridges may well have been constructed for the use of foot passengers only, perhaps over the brook running through Budleigh Salterton. In Devon such a bridge was commonly distinguished by the name 'clapper' or 'clam'. It was simply constructed, consisting of two pieces of granite or wooden planks laid on top of a pile of stones.

Floods towards the latter end of 1810 caused damage to the road at Salterton, destroying the bridge there which had been constructed in 1805. It would seem that the workmanship and/or materials that had been applied to this bridge were poor to say the least, as a mason called John French was paid £9.6s.6d. for the 'deficiency of erecting a new bridge at Budley Salterton'.

At a meeting of the inhabitants held by public notice on 27 December 1810 it was announced that a rate of not less than £150 was to be raised to cover repairs to a storm-damaged bridge. The rate was to be levied through the property rate, over two years, and was not to exceed more than 6d. in the pound. The money collected was to be given to the surveyor of the highways with the mandate to build 'a good strong bridge at Salterton' and carry out other repairs there, so it would appear that a new bridge was to replace the one damaged in the storm. The brook on the lower side of the bridge, on the east side of the water, was to be fenced in, whilst the road on the east side of the brook was to be 'filled up' from the bridge to the beach. The resulting bridge was to be fit for all horses and carriages to pass over. The money raised by the rate was not to be used to repair the road any further than 20ft beyond the bridge, nor was it to be spent on the roads in other parts of the parish.

At a Vestry meeting held on 24 January 1811, it was decided to increase the rate agreed on 27 December 1810 to £200. This increase was on the condition that Mr Green, presumably the contractor building the bridge, carried his own plan into execution and that Lord Rolle's contribution of £100 was added to the agreed sum of the £200.

Upon the new brick bridge at Salterton being completed, a 22ft stone wall was built from the south corner of the bridge, towards the village. The wall was built on the orders of Lord Rolle, at the expense of the parish.

The Brook

The brook running through Budleigh Salterton presented ongoing problems inasmuch that it often had to be cleaned out. However, action was not always taken as entries in the Vestry minutes book indicate.

During February 1860, a letter addressed to the waywarden, Mr Strickland, from a Mr Wrentmore demanded that he:

remove forthwith the shingle deposited in the water course below the weir towards the sea and which prevented the drainage of my houses called South Promenade situated in Budleigh Salterton.

At a meeting convened to debate the contents of the letter, the ratepayers considered they had nothing to do with Mr Wrentmore's situation; it was therefore resolved not to comply with his demand. It would seem the decision taken at the meeting stood, as no further references to his complaint appear.

The Vestry did, however, find themselves deliberating the necessity of cleaning and draining the brook at Budleigh Salterton in October 1863. A committee was formed to establish the best means of carrying out the work and delivered a report on the matter in March of the following year. Mr Rolle consented to the drainage of the brook from the head of the weir to Humphries Bridge and five tenders were received from contractors keen to do the job.

'A committee of gentleman' was then appointed to go round the houses in Salterton to raise the sum of £128.10s. towards defraying the total expenses of £250. The owners of house properties in Salterton undertook to rate themselves at 1s.6d. in the pound, thus raising £115. The outstanding balance of £13.10s. was guaranteed by Mr Smith. A request was made for the remaining £122 to be contributed by the Highways Board.

The cleaning and draining of the brook was undertaken by Mr Strickland at the total cost of £248.9s.5d., leaving an unexpended sum of £1.10s.7d. It was decided that this remaining sum of money should be put towards defraying the costs of erecting weirs in different parts of the brook.

Sanitary Committee

Governments became more preoccupied with public health during the course of the nineteenth century. After the cholera outbreak of 1831, health became associated with clean water and sanitation. The Public Health Act of 1848 resulted in Public Health Boards with the power to raise money for water supplies and sewer systems for areas with an above-average death rate; this was eventually applied to all remaining parts of the country.

Entries in the Vestry minutes book from the period 1851–71 reflect this new awareness about disease and health and its consequences for the inhabitants of East Budleigh.

In 1855 a Nuisance Removal Committee was appointed for the whole parish. This committee was probably formed as a result of the cholera outbreak of 1853–54 but, unfortunately, there is no record of their activities. Their task may simply have been to ensure that sources of drinking-water were kept clean. In 1865 another outbreak of cholera was feared in England, resulting in the appointment of another committee in August of that year to 'inspect and report on any nuisances in the parish which may be injurious to health'. The following month East Budleigh and Knowle were reported as being the source of 'nuisances' but no indication was given as to their exact nature.

In March 1860 it was decided to erect two water pumps, at the cost of £5 each, for the general use of the inhabitants. One pump was to be situated on the town side and one on the land side.

Members appointed to the Sanitary Committee in July 1866 were Messrs Caseley, G. Bence, W. Strickland, H. Carter, G. Hill, J. Walters, J. Smith and J. Cann for Salterton and Knowle. In October 1876 it was suggested that Budleigh Salterton should form its own Local Board of Health, however, this proposal was rejected.

Office of Cattle Overseer

The cattle plague fright during the winter of 1865–66 affected England to such an extent that the Devon Quarter Sessions established a Cattle Plague Committee, whilst parishes around the county elected cattle overseers to ensure that no cattle came into Devon. A licence had to be obtained by those wishing to move cattle and all markets and fairs were closed. Areas which had been declared infected could only be given the all clear by the Quarter Sessions.

The following cattle overseers were nominated and appointed at a Vestry meeting in February 1866: Mr Samuel Pile of Kersbrook; Mr Cockman of Pulhayes Farm, East Budleigh; William Walters of Little Knowle; J. Carter of East Budleigh; H. Leatt of Knowle; E. Harding of Budleigh Salterton; B. Bastin of Tidwell Barton; J. Lawrence of Hayes Barton. All were yeoman, with the exception of E. Harding who was a dairyman.

As there are no further entries regarding the appointed cattle overseers, we can only assume that the 'cattle plague fright' must have been just that, a fright.

References:

J. Cannon (ed.), *The Oxford Companion to British History* (Oxford, Oxford University Press, 2002).

Devon County Prison (HMP Exeter): Receiving Books of various dates.

Devon Record Office: Box D12/30; East Budleigh 1180A/PW1 Churchwardens Account Book 1664–1784, PW2 1839–40: East Budleigh 1180A/PO1 Overseers Account Books 1693–1746, PO2 1768–86, PO3 1787–1806, PO4 1828–1836; East Budleigh 1180A/add2/PW15 Accounts, Rates etc., 1560–1705; East Budleigh 1180A/add3/PV1 Vestry meetings 1851–71; East Budleigh 1180A/PS1 Highway Rates and Accounts 1803-33, PS2 1833–63; Overseers of the Poor, East Budleigh, Catalogue for Apprenticeships, Removal Orders, Settlement Examinations, Bastardy Orders, various references as PO503/504/505/511/514/515/519/725; Box D12/30; Quarter Sessions (Midsummer Sessions 1866) H586.

Funeral Furnishing Account Books, various dates. (Palmers' Funeral Service, Budleigh Salterton).

J. Richardson, *The Local Historian's Encyclopedia*, (New Barnet, Historical Publications, 1986).

W.E. Tate, *The Parish Chest: A Study of the Records of Parochial Administration in England*, (Cambridge, Cambridge University Press, 1946).

Trewman's *Exeter Flying Post*, various dates.

Westcountry Studies Library: newspaper cuttings.

Chapter 4

◇

Smugglers and Preventive Officers

Smuggling through the Ages

Prior to looking at the smugglers and preventive officers local to Budleigh Salterton, we shall look briefly at smuggling through the ages. During the time of Ethelred II (who was king of England during the years 978–1016) a toll charge came about, allowing foreigners to trade in this country. It was with the advent of this toll that smugglers came into being, evading payment of the toll by avoiding the officials appointed to collect it. By its very nature smuggling was an exciting business. The scoundrels of society were drawn to it, lured by the promise of fiscal gain and the thrills associated with the danger of being caught by the revenue men.

Smugglers believed that the state should not interfere in what people bought and sold. Whilst they had the support of certain fractions of the public and were often viewed as loveable rogues rather than dangerous criminals, they were, however, guilty of transgressing the law. Whatever the rights and wrongs of smuggling, Oppenheim took a practical view on the matter in his book *The Maritime History of Devon* when he wrote 'whatever its moral aspect [smuggling] turned out first-class seamen'.

Towards the end of the thirteenth century a custom was placed on wool, a mainstay of the English economy that was being exported to the Continent. Wool thus became a commodity for the smugglers, as did all the other wares subject to taxation.

During the seventeenth and eighteenth centuries smuggling became a popular pursuit. Under the cover of darkness, goods were brought inland from boats and dispersed amongst safe houses and lock-ups with the aid of willing helpers who distracted the local revenue officers. Items smuggled included brandy, wine, cloth, silk handkerchiefs, playing cards and other diverse goods, as well as many household commodities such as tea. As the smugglers' wares were cheaper than those legally obtainable, the public was most appreciative.

Sherbrook Chine, 1930s.   (STEVE RICHARDSON)

Sherbrook Chine Steps, 1920s.   (STEVE RICHARDSON)

Smuggling and Corruption

In order to combat smuggling, revenue cruisers patrolled the waters around ports as early as the fifteenth century, but as long stretches of coastal waters lay unprotected the smugglers could easily continue their pursuit. As customs officials were poorly paid, many of them were not adverse to accepting bribes. Corruption was also rife amongst the personnel on board naval vessels, called to assist the customs men with their duties. Customs officials at Budleigh Salterton were subjected to improper conduct by those who were supposed to assist them in their lawful duty, as reported by the collector of excise duty at Exeter in 1791:

a Customs boatman at Budleigh Salterton had suffered ill-usage when a lieutenant and some of the crew of HMS Narcissus *seized 40 casks and a boat from him!*

By the seventeenth century the Board of Customs had a small fleet of its own but it could still call upon the assistance of the Royal Navy to help catch those evading excise duty.

Preventive Officers

In 1698, riding officers were established in Kent and Sussex but did not cover the rest of the English coast until the end of the eighteenth century. Their duty was to prevent the inland movement of goods smuggled past the revenue cruisers at sea and the customs officers at the ports. From 1673 those who held a civil or military office had to produce a Sacrament Certificate signed by a minister, churchwardens and two witnesses to confirm that the Sacrament of the Lord's Supper had been received by them. From two such certificates we learn that in 1715 Edward Hurley was a 'riding officer, weigher and searcher at Budleigh Salterton in the port of Exeter' and that in 1732, Joseph Turncock from East Budleigh was a custom-house officer, although it is not stated where he was stationed.

In 1809 the Preventive Water Guard (commonly known as 'preventive boatmen') was established. Based in watch houses around the coast, they were superintended by a chief officer who was normally a Royal Navy lieutenant with boat crews patrolling the coastal water in the area. In 1822 the revenue cruisers, the riding officers and the Preventive Water Guard were amalgamated to form the Coastguard.

The instructions to the Coastguard in 1829 read as follows:

All Officers and Persons employed in the Coast Guard,

are to bear in mind that the sole object of their appointment is the Protection of the Revenue: and that their utmost endeavours are therefore to be used to prevent the landing of uncustomed goods, and to seize all persons, vessels, boats, cattle, and carriages, in any way employed in Smuggling and all goods liable to be forfeited by law.

Every Person in the Coast Guard is to consider it his first and most important object to secure the person of the Smuggler; and the reward granted for each smuggler convicted, or the share of the penalty recovered from him, will be paid (on the Certificate of the Inspecting Commander) to the person or persons by whom the smuggler is absolutely taken and secured, and not to the crew in general.

In opposition to the smugglers on the coast of East Devon were customs officers and preventive boatman stationed at Exeter, Exmouth, Budleigh Salterton and Lyme Regis. They were supported by a small number of unarmed riding officers based at Lympstone, Sidmouth, Branscombe, Beer and Seaton. As a consequence of the suspicious death of the riding officer at Beer in 1752 the 'Sitter' (watchman) and preventive boatman at Budleigh Salterton were issued with a pair of horse pistols and two 'hangers with guards' (swords).

Revenue men were, however, not always at odds with smugglers. At the Exmouth Regatta in August 1834 they competed with each other in the revenue boat match. This was won by the *Adder Cutter* – of where is not stated – which beat boats from the Exmouth, Salterton and Dawlish stations.

A New Customs Watch House

A lease between the Rt Hon. John Lord Rolle, Baron Rolle of Stevenstone and George Delavaud of the Customs House London, secretary to the Hon. Commissioners of His Majesty's Customs, signed and dated 4 May 1819, mentions a new customs watch house, built on the site of the old watch house at Budleigh Salterton. The new watch house was bound on the north and east by a hedge; the south boundary comprised 26ft of 'sunk stone wall', built to protect the watch house from the sea. The lease was for a term of 99 years or three lives, with a yearly rent of £3.2s. The collector at Exeter had to do 'suit and service' at the court of Rolle i.e. attend the lord's manor court and carry out certain duties. All costs and charges to maintain the building and sunk stone wall in front of the premises were to be paid by customs officials.

A further condition stipulated that should any ship or vessel become stranded or wrecked on the

The Flagstaff, Budleigh Salterton, 1930s.

(STEVE RICHARDSON)

coast of East Budleigh, the customs officials were to 'use their utmost endeavours to preserve the same and the lives of the persons belonging thereto'.

Smuggling in and around Budleigh Salterton

Evidence of smuggling in and around Budleigh Salterton is quite plentiful. Even two clergymen from East Budleigh, Revd Matthew Munday and Revd Ambrose Stapleton, were reputedly involved in smuggling over the period 1741–1852. Local smugglers, along with the aforementioned clergymen, supposedly planned their escapades in the parish room in the rectory. Smuggled goods were stashed in secret hiding-places in the north and south walls of the fifteenth-century rectory, known at the time of writing as Vicar's Mead. According to local legend, there were many such hiding-places in East Budleigh, including the church:

> There was scarcely a house along the coast, or a farm-house, or inn within easy distance, but had its cellar or 'private place,' or 'hide' as these receptacles were called, and the ingenuity displayed in their construction was certainly very wonderful. So admirably were they contrived in many instances, that on change of owner-ship their very existence has been unsuspected, until the subsidence of a beam, or alterations in the house, have laid open cavities which doubtless held many a good tub of brandy in their time.

One winter's night during December 1822 officers of the Coastguard captured a boat containing 128 kegs of spirit. Nothing further transpires of this seizure but doubtless, the festive season was lacking a certain something for many parishioners that year!

During another incident, Philip Hodnett, a boatman in the service of the customs stationed at Budleigh Salterton, was 'violently assaulted and obstructed' by a gang of unknown smugglers at

Chisselbury, East of Otter Head in November 1824. A reward of £50, to be paid on conviction, was offered by the customs commissioners to any person apprehending the offenders.

In February 1825 the custom boat crew stationed at Budleigh Salterton found 60 kegs of spirits in Budleigh Salterton bay. In December of the same year, a Budleigh Salterton carrier, Mr Alderman Floud, had a box consigned to his care stolen from his cart, whilst it was being delivered to Exeter. The box was found opened in the possession of two men, Taylor and Knowles. To the abashment of the carrier, the box was found to contain a keg of smuggled liquor with an invoice. Taylor and Knowles walked free from their hearing at the petty sessions as the carrier failed to appear to give his evidence.

Customs officials pulled off a coup in February 1834. A boat containing 141 tubs of spirit with four French and one English hand on board was seized off Fasye [sic] Common, 2 miles east of Budleigh Salterton. Shortly afterwards, at the same position, a sloop of 36 tons burthen with an Englishman and Frenchman on board was seized by the crew of the cutter *Sprightly* from Exmouth. For customs officials it was the largest haul of contraband spirits that had been seized in the district for a long time.

On 3 January 1833 officials were not quite as lucky. A French smuggler ran his cargo of 100 tubs of spirits at Ladram Bay. A preventive officer from Sidmouth, accompanied by a colleague from Budleigh Salterton, endeavoured to prevent the landing but they were overpowered by 70 men who had come to assist the French. One man attempted to remove six tubs and a flagon. On being ordered not to do so, he rushed the Sidmouth Coastguard who reacted by firing his pistol; the ball passed through the crown of another man's hat. The Coastguard was overpowered, his cutlass and pistol were taken from him and he was then dreadfully beaten up. His Salterton comrade had his arm broken. One of the men impeached several of his fellow smugglers who lived in and around Sidford. They were taken into custody for examination by magistrates.

Arrests were also made on 22 June 1839 when the preventive crew of the Budleigh Salterton Coastguard station seized five men and a considerable number of tubs near Brandy Head, Otterton. The men were put before magistrates, Mr W. Hull and Mr R. Harding on 29 June at Exmouth. The five men, unnamed, were convicted after a long and searching investigation by the magistrates. Each man was fined £100 and in default of non-payment, they were to be confined within the walls of the county gaol at Exeter.

A Smuggler's Song

By Rudyard Kipling (From *Puck of Puck's Hill*)

If you wake at midnight, and hear a horse's feet, Don't go drawing back the blind, or looking in the street.
Them that ask no questions isn't told a lie.
Watch the wall, my darling, while the Gentlemen go by!

Five-and-twenty ponies,
Trotting through the dark –
Brandy for the Parson,
'Baccy for the Clerk;
Laces for a lady, letters for a spy,
And watch the wall, my darling, while the Gentlemen go by!

Running round the woodlump if you chance to find
Little barrels, roped and tarred, all full of brandy-wine;
Don't you shout to come and look, nor use 'em for your play.
Put the brushwood back again – and they'll be gone next day!

If you see the stable-door setting open wide;
If you see a tired horse lying down inside;
If your mother mends a coat cut about and tore;
If the lining's wet and warm – don't you ask no more!

If you meet King George's men, dressed in blue and red,
You be careful what you say, and mindful what is said.
If they call you 'pretty maid', and chuck you 'neath the chin,
Don't you tell where no one is, nor yet where no one's been!

Knocks and footsteps round the house – whistles after dark –
You've no call for running out till the house-dogs bark.
Trusty's here, and Pincher's here, and see how dumb they lie –
They don't fret to follow when the Gentlemen go by!

If you do as you've been told, likely there's a chance,
You'll be given a dainty doll, all the way from France,
With a cap of Valenciennes, and a velvet hood –
A present from the Gentlemen, along o' being good!

Five-and-twenty ponies,
Trotting through the dark –
Brandy for the Parson,
'Baccy for the Clerk;
Them that asks no questions isn't told a lie –
Watch the wall, my darling, while the Gentlemen go by!

It would be intresting to discover more about the seizure, especially as one of the justices made a point of mentioning:

the credit due to, and the great intrepidity shown by John Jones, of the coast guardsmen, by whose presence of mind, certainly bloodshed and probably even lives were saved.

Unfortunately the exact nature of the actions undertaken by the intrepid John Jones are not revealed.

Smugglers did, however, manage to get the better of the preventive men whilst transporting a number of brandy tubs landed at Budleigh Salterton in 1858. The tubs were being taken to Woodhead Farm, between Branscombe and Beer, via Trow Hill on the A3052. Upon being alerted to the presence of preventive men, 18-year-old George Bray threw the tubs into a ditch where they lay undiscovered by the officials. They were later recovered and taken to Woodhead Farm, the home of George's father, Samuel Bray, as originally planned. Budleigh Salterton to Beer was a short journey for the Brays, they had been known to move smuggled goods to Beer from North Devon.

The smugglers William Mutter and Charles Blackmore were not quite as successful. In the early hours of a Monday morning in July 1857, their boat was noticed by Coastguard Richard Jago from the Exmouth station who was on his beat at Straight Point. Jago was joined by William Wragg, a Coastguard from Budleigh Salterton. After watching Mutter and Blackmore illegally land contraband spirit, which they then concealed under the cliffs, the two Coastguards descended to the beach. On seeing the preventive men carrying out a search of the area, Mutter and Blackmore hid themselves but to no avail – they were soon discovered. The preventive men fired an alarm, after which Mr Prawle and his men, also stationed at Budleigh Salterton, arrived on the scene to assist their colleagues. A total of 41 tubs and four flagons of brandy were found along with other articles. William Mutter and Charles Blackmore were then committed to the county gaol for safe custody, charged with illegally landing 41 tubs of brandy, until their case came up before the Exmouth magistrates. The bench found both men guilty as charged. They were fined £700 with six months' imprisonment in lieu of non-payment of the fines. As they were unable to pay the fines, they were committed to gaol.

The Case of Rattenbury and Bird

On 1 December 1835 during the evening of what had been a wintry, windswept day, John Batchelor, chief boatman of the Coastguard at Budleigh Salterton was out on the shore, looking seaward. He was watching out for vessels which looked as if they might be participating in a smuggling run. At about midnight he spotted a vessel, which was 6 or 7 miles off, coming in from the sea with another boat astern of her. The manner in which the vessel tacked on and off instantly aroused Batchelor's suspicions so he reported the matter to his commanding officer, Lieutenant Clay.

William Noble Clay, with the rank and pay of a Naval Lieutenant, had been at Budleigh Salterton for nearly three years. It was his duty to prevent smuggling, so when Batchelor informed him of the suspicious vessel, he went to see it for himself. Upon observing the movement of the vessel, Clay came to the same conclusion as his chief boatman. Clay ordered Batchelor to keep his eye on the vessel whilst he himself headed west, to a cliff where he would be able to see more.

At about half past one that night, Batchelor saw a boat near the shore where there was a lot of surf and a great number of men gathered. Hearing a report of firearms he made his way towards the men, firing his pistol as a signal.

Clay in the meantime had sighted a number of men on the beach from his vantage point on the cliff. He signalled by firing his pistol twice, this being the report of firearms heard by Batchelor. Shortly after, Clay was approached by a group of men and another group emerged from behind a bank. With shouts of 'Seize him! Give it to him!' they closed in on Clay who informed them who he was but to no avail. They took hold of him, bound his hands behind his back and then tied his legs together. Armed with guns, pistols and bludgeons some of the men proceeded to beat Clay, who was in no position to escape. It was a bright moonlit night and Clay was able to notice what two of the men assaulting him were wearing. He was also able to identify one of them as the ringleader, later recalling 'He was so close to me as at times to touch me.' The man, who had a pistol in his left trouser pocket with the muzzle on view, was William Rattenbury of Beer. The second man, Henry Bird, was also armed with a gun.

Clay told the men to desist from beating him at which juncture someone cried 'Give it to him!' and his pistol and cutlass were removed from his person. When he demanded that his pistol be returned to him, pointing to the one in Rattenbury's pocket, Rattenbury retorted that it was his own, adding 'd.....d well loaded it is!'

Batchelor arrived on the scene to find Clay calling for mercy, surrounded by 60–70 men. Unable to get near him, Batchelor 'burnt a blue light' and fired his pistol, whereupon he was attacked himself. Brandishing his cutlass he managed to escape and ran into the village of Budleigh Salterton to summon help. Baker Henry Perriam agreed to assist Batchelor, accompanying him back to the scene of the incident, but the two men were still unable to reach Clay. Batchelor fired his pistol. One of the men grabbed Perriam's waistcoat whilst another, Bird, put his gun to Perriam's head. Fortunately, Batchelor managed to disperse the smugglers by firing a blue light.

Clay and Batchelor went to the smugglers' boat and removed 52 kegs of brandy; these were then passed to Richard Davis who delivered them to the Custom House at Exeter.

Allen Walters, a surgeon at Exmouth, examined Clay and Batchelor the following day. Lieutenant Clay's right shoulder was bruised 'from the blow of a bludgeon' to such a degree, that he could not use his arm, thus he was unfit for duty. Bachelor's left hand was 'a good deal swollen'. Clay informed a court some three months later that 'I suffer from the blows even now'.

Lieutenant Clay imparted a description of Rattenbury to William Glover, a commission boatman at Exmouth. Rattenbury was apprehended and taken into custody by Glover on the following Saturday at Exmouth, where 'the affray was common talk'.

Edward Manico, a Lieutenant in the Coastguard service, apprehended Bird at Buckerell five days after the incident, on 6 December. Manico informed Bird that he had a warrant to search his house and that he also had a warrant against him for assaulting an officer at Salterton.

In March 1836, at the Nisi Prius Court at Exeter, Rattenbury and Bird stood before Mr Justice Littledale, indicted that 'with force and violence, they assaulted and obstructed Lieutenant Clay and John Batchelor, officers, employed in the preventive service, when engaged in the execution of their duty'. The prosecution related the facts of the case to the jury.

Mr Cockburn and Mr Merivale appeared for the defendants. Mr Cockburn addressed the jury claiming that the prosecution relied solely on Lieutenant Clay's somewhat dubious identification of the defendants. Under cross-examination, Clay told the court that he was only able to identify Rattenbury and Bird, none of the other men. Batchelor had not identified anyone, nor had Perriam.

The defence counsel then called witnesses who said that both defendants were at home during the whole of the night in question. One such witness was David Starling, a fisherman from Beer, who said he had been at sea all his life. Although he had served in the Navy for ten years he professed not to know what smuggling was. Rattenbury lived at Beer with his mother-in-law and was allegedly seen by Starling at 9p.m. on the night in question, whilst discussing securing the boats from the gale and the surf.

Another witness was Richard Leman, also a fisherman from Beer, who knew both Rattenbury and Starling. On 1 December Leman allegedly saw Rattenbury and Starling standing at Starling's door, 'it was nine o'clock up or down'.

A third witness, Patience Newton, also lived at Beer and worked for Rattenbury's father. She was no relation but worked with Fanny and Mary Ann Rattenbury. She said that she saw Mr Rattenbury at 10p.m. on the night in question.

John Rattenbury of Beer, better known as Jack, was the father of the defendant. He said that it was very windy on 1 December. He went to bed about 9p.m. that night and he heard his son come in. He said he knew the day of the month because he went to church every Sunday. Jack added he had always been liked by every man and had been a smuggler, but would not take a false oath to save his wife or child.

William Williams, a cordwainer, was a parish constable of Beer. He had been to sea, on the French coast and among the Dutch men and had tried Dutch gin, which he liked when he could get it. Despite his experience of going to sea, he also claimed not to 'know what you call smuggling'. He had seen William Rattenbury on the night of 1 December, at 10.45p.m., on the street at Beer going towards his home.

Also from Beer, 77-year-old Sarah Clarke said that the defendant William Rattenbury was married to her daughter; the couple had lived in her house since their marriage. She remembered the night of Tuesday 1 December as it was blowing such a gale. That night, Rattenbury came in about 11p.m. and had bread, cheese, onions and cider for his supper. He then went to bed upstairs where he spoke to his wife. Clarke insisted that although her memory was 'very shallow' and she did not recollect all that had passed, she was sure that Rattenbury was an innocent man.

After the six witnesses for Rattenbury had given their evidence, William Bird's witnesses were called. The first was Daniel Salter, who had lived at Buckerell for 40 years. He said that William Bird, a married man, lived at Buckerell in a lone cottage. On 1 December Bird had called on Salter at around 9p.m., just as he was going to bed.

The second witness was William Newton, a tailor, who lived at Honiton. Bird had called on him at about 3p.m. on 1 December to buy some cloth to make his little boy some clothes. On arriving at Bird's house at 7a.m. the next morning, Newton saw him putting on his boots. There was nothing particular in the appearance of Bird or his clothes to indicate that he had been up all night.

The jury, however, decided that Rattenbury and Bird were indeed at Budleigh Salterton on the night of 1 December, not at home as they and their witnesses professed; both defendants were found guilty as charged. Mr Justice Littledale gave such a sentence as to ensure that they would not return home for seven years: they were transported for their turpitude.

Local Coastguards

In the 1851 census there is mention of a Lieutenant William Hole, who gave his status as 'Seat in the Royal Navy Employed in the Coastguard Service', as the Coastguard Commander at Budleigh Salterton. He lived in Victoria Place. James Ahern was Chief Boatman, he lived in Chapel Street. In addition to these two men, five other Coastguards resided in Victoria Place, two in Chapel Street and three in Fore Street. Two superannuated Coastguards lived in Fore Street, with another living in Victoria Place. One of the Coastguards had been born in Budleigh Salterton, two others had been born at Littleham and Exmouth. The remainder came from as far afield as Chatham and Ireland. One of the reasons for having people from outside the area employed in the Coastguard was that outsiders were less likely to owe favours to locals, thus making it harder for their position to be compromised

In January 1877 an accident resulted in the drowning of Thomas Cusack, a 35-year-old Coastguard. The County Coroner held an inquest at the Rolle Arms Hotel to investigate how his death came about. Cusack had been ferrying two other Coastguards, detailed for duty, across the River Otter. Whilst they attempted to cross the river near its mouth, the tide turned, due to a freshet caused by recent heavy rains. The boat, with Cusack at the oars, was taken out to sea and dashed against rocks. Russell and Griffin, the two passengers, managed to swim away from the boat. Their cries of dolour were heard by W. and E. Bucknill and Mr Cooper, who rescued the Coastguards with ropes, 'just in time'.

The deceased had been able to swim, so his drowning was attributed to his body being jammed

Coastguards carrying out their breechers buoy drill at Otterton Point, 1930s. (NICK LOMAN COLLECTION)

between the boat and the rocks. He was found the following morning 'nearly covered with beach'.

The jury, who returned a verdict of accidental death, gave their fees to the widow of the deceased and remarked that 'high praise' was due to the men who had rescued the two surviving Coastguards.

Another Budleigh Salterton Coastguard was immortalised by author Stephen Reynolds in the book *A Poor Man's House*, first published in 1908. Reynolds based the fictitious character, Ned Luscombe, on Jim Battishill, whom he had met in 1903.

The Battishills moved into the Coastguard cottages on 12 May 1903, and shortly after their 11-month-old son died. The fact that they had suffered such a terrible loss did not deter them from helping others, especially those shunned by society, as the following extract from the book reveals:

a girl crippled in such a way that though she could walk all right she could not get up again if thrown down. A fellow got her down, put her in the family way and left her lying there. Salterton thereupon gave her the cold shoulder.

The Battishills, however, invited the girl to their house for tea, after which she visited every day for a long time.

Local Coastguards proved themselves worthy of praise in October 1857, when a total of 99 Coastguard volunteers from Sidmouth, Budleigh Salterton, Topsham, Exmouth and Exeter mustered at Exmouth. They embarked on board the *Nimble*, cutter of Exmouth, and the *Lion*, cutter of Dartmouth, and were conveyed to Portland, before being drafted to ships of the line. They were described as 'a fine body consisting chiefly of men inured to hardships of the sea'.

References:

T.N. Brushfield, 'The Church of All Saints, East Budleigh', *Transactions Devonshire Association* Part III, (1894).

Devon Records Office: 96m/Box 41/4C, Quarter Sessions, QS/21/1715/188 and 1732/48.

R. Gutteridge, *Dorset Smugglers* (Salisbury, Dorset Publishing Company, 1984).

S. Reynolds *A Poor Man's House* (Tiverton, Halsgrove, 2001).

J. Richardson, *The Local Historian's Encyclopedia* (New Barnet, Historical Publications, 1986).

Trewman's *Exeter Flying Post*, various dates.

M. Waugh, *Smuggling in Devon & Cornwall 1700–1850* (Newbury, Countryside Books, 1999).

White's *1850 Directory of Devon*, (New York, A.M. Kelly, 1968).

Westcountry Studies Library: newspaper cuttings.

Patrons: Her Majesty The Queen
Her Majesty Queen Elizabeth, The Queen Mother

ROYAL NATIONAL LIFE-BOAT INSTITUTION

Founded 1824   Supported entirely by Voluntary Contributions

CHAIRMAN: ADMIRAL SIR WILFRID WOODS, G.B.E., K.C.B., D.S.O.
DEPUTY CHAIRMEN: COMMANDER F.R.H. SWANN, O.B.E., R.N.V.R.
LIEUT-COMMANDER THE HON. GREVILLE HOWARD, V.R.D., R.N.R.
TREASURER: THE DUKE OF NORTHUMBERLAND, K.G., D.C.L.
SECRETARY: STIRLING WHORLOW, ESQ., O.B.E.
CHIEF INSPECTOR OF LIFE-BOATS: LIEUT-COMMANDER W. L. G. DUTTON, R.D., R.N.R.

Telephone: 01-730 0031

Telegrams: Shorescue, London, S.W.1   LIFE-BOAT HOUSE, 42 GROSVENOR GARDENS, LONDON, S.W.1

O/D/DA

12th August 1969.

L. Lomas Esq.,
19 Meadow Road,
Budleigh Salterton,
Devon.

Dear Sir,

The report of the incident which took place on the 29th July at Budleigh Salterton has been received and read with interest, and I write to let you know that it has been decided to grant you a monetary award of £1.10.0. This is assessed on the same scale as you would have received had you been a member of a life-boat or inshore rescue boat crew on a similar service.

I enclose our cheque for this amount. No acknowledgment is necessary.

Yours faithfully,

M.S.Porcher.
Assistant Secretary (Organisation)

A monetary reward, 1969. (N. Loman was the recipient of this payment, not L. Lomas.)

(NICK LOMAN COLLECTION)

Chapter 5

◇

Lime and Manganese

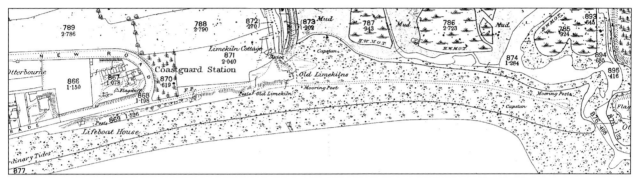

The 1890 Ordnance Survey map (scale: 25in to 1 mile; reduced) showing the position of the limekilns.

(CLINTON DEVON ESTATES)

Polwhele, writing in 1797, informs us that 'the cliffs on each side of Torbay, Berryhead, and Hope's-nose, and so round to Babbacombe, are entirely of limestone'. It was from this area that limestone was brought in a (lime-)stone boat, owned by Lord Rolle, to his limekilns at Budleigh Salterton. The burning agent, culm, was brought from Wales by a boat belonging to a Brixham dealer. Lord Rolle doubtless operated the limekilns to benefit his own estate.

Using Lime on the Land

The Romans were the first to burn lime in this country, although limekilns associated with them have mainly been found near building sites. Tristram Risdon, the Devonshire historian, writing in the early part of the seventeenth century, seems to think, however, that the burning of lime came about in his time, for he relates that:

Of late a new invention has sprung up, and been prac-
tised, by burning lime, and incorporating it for a
season with earth, and then spread upon arable land,
hath produced a plentiful increase in all sorts of grain
among us, where formally such never grew in any
living man's memory.

From a lease dated 1763 we find that lime was

regarded as an important commodity for ensuring the sustained productivity of land used for crops. The lease, concerning a Devonshire farm, informed the prospective lessee, amongst its many dos and don'ts, of the following:

[The lessee] shall and will bring or cause to be brought
into every acre of the said premises that shall be Tilled
or broken up for Tillage Fifty Bushells of good coale
burnt stone Lyme of Double Winchester measures or
Forty Horse teams of small Lyme... and so proportion-
ally after that rate into any less quantity than an acre of
the said premises that shall be so Tilled or broken up for
Tillage and there spread and cast abroad the same
according to good Husbandry.

As for the benefits of spreading lime on the land Polwhele remarks:

Various have been the conjectures as to its melioration of
the soil. Tull says, lime nourishes plants... But I have
always been of the opinion, that one great advantage
accruing from dressing with lime, is the destruction of
the grub, slug, and worm... Another method by which
land may be benefited by lime is, that... if there be any...
acid juices of the soil... lime will attract the acid ...

Up until the twentieth century, lime was regarded as a fertiliser. The advantages of using lime on the land,

93

A engraving of Budleigh Salterton foreshore, dating from c.1835, showing limekilns (to the right) *in operation.*
(PETER MCMILLAN)

Fred Gooding with Silver Jubilee, Moor Lane, 1933. (KATH GOODING)

Albert Heard (left) *and Ted Hallet with the silver cup presented by Lord Clinton for the champion beast at East Budleigh Christmas Show, 1930s.*
(KATH GOODING)

however, came not from its properties as a fertaliser, but from the fact that it neutralised any acid contained in the soil.

From the publication *Mates' Illustrated Budleigh Salterton* we find that the limekilns supplied farms and others with lime up until 1875.

The Lime-Burning Process

The lime-burning process at a Plymouth limekiln, was described in 1786 by a commanding Royal Engineer as follows:

After the Stones are Quarried and broke with a large Maul (about 18 or 20 lbs.) to a portable size fit to be lifted on a small Horse, they are carried upon the Kiln Bed, and there broke with small Mauls (about 4 lbs.) to a size fit for burning, none of which should exceed 3 pounds in weight. The Wood is then to be laid on the Ground under the Grating at the bottom of the Kiln, which should be Furze or other small Wood, on which a layer of small Culm is laid, and then a layer of Limestones, and so on Alternately with the Culm and Limestones till you get 8 or 9 Tiers high, when the Fire is to be lighted, and when the Wood is consumed, the Limestones in the Middle of the Kiln will naturally sink, a small quantity of Culm is then to be added, and the Limestones in the Kiln brought to a level with the long Poker... This being done a layer of Culm is put on, and on that a layer of Limestones, and which is alternately repeated, till the Kiln is three quarters full, which will be in the course of 4 or 5 Days, at the end of which time some Lime will be produced, and then the shifting Bars... are to be introduced across the top of the three fixed Bars... at the Bottom of the Kiln; this the Limeburners say saves a considerable quantity of Culm. The Kiln is now to be gradually filled with a layer of Culm and Limestones alternately, when it is considered to be in a full state of Burning, and will generally produce between 60 and 70 Winchester Bushels of Lime a Day; this however depends in some measure on the Wind which prevails at the time, for the higher the wind is, the greater will be the quantity of Lime produced.

The breaking of the Limestones, when brought on the Kiln Head, to the size proper for burning, is performed by two Men who constantly attend by Day, in order to keep the Kiln well supplied with Stone, and to remove its produce, which is done every Morning.

The Culm made use of for burning the Lime must be of the smallest kind, and should there be any Stones in it, they must be separated from it by a Skreen. The proportion of Culm for burning, is about 7 Winchesters to 25 of Lime.

Doubtless the method of lime burning at the Budleigh Salterton kilns was carried out in a very similar way to that as given above.

The Salterton Limekilns

From a conveyance dated 1 October 1759 we find that provided John Walter of Stevenstone paid 5s. to Philip and John Parkhouse, executors of Mary Gould of Littleham, they would lease him for a term of one year and a peppercorn rent:

the moiety of the lime kilns and lime pit with the plot of ground on Salterton beach formerly in the possession of Roger Gould deceased afterward in the possession of his grandson Roger Gould also deceased and since in the possession of Mary Gould together with all the ways, paths, passages and appurtenances whatsoever to the moiety of the lime kiln.

We can see that the limekiln at Budleigh Salterton had been in operation for some time prior to the date of the sale of the moiety, as it had previously leased for three lives.

A moiety of the limekiln was again to change hands. On 7 May 1762 Thomas Weeks of East Budleigh 'now being in possession of the moiety of the limekiln situated on Salterton beach' transferred his moiety to the Revd John Glubb of Bicton.

Shortly following this exchange a lease was signed between John Walter of Stevenstone, Esquire, George Cockram, Gentleman, and the following three men from Budleigh Salterton: Richard Scott, Mariner; Edward Harris, Yeoman; William Farr, one of the boatmen belonging to the customs of the port of Exon. The lease concerned 'All that Lime Kiln situated on Salterton Beach within the parish of East Budleigh' from 24 June 1762 for a ten-year term. A yearly rent of £5 was to be paid in four payments 'at the four most usual Feasts in the year' i.e. at Michaelmas, Christmas, Easter and Midsummer.

The lessees were to keep the kilns 'sufficiently repaired and amended as required'. The four men were also to make an agreement with John Duke to pay 1s. for each boat of limestone that was to be landed on the beach to be burnt in the kilns. After due payment of the rent, the men were to 'lawfully, peaceably and quietly hold and enjoy the lime kilns without let, trouble, interruption, contradiction and denial from John Walter'.

After a period of 33 years passed from the signing of the lease, it was considered necessary to repair the limekiln. It also seems that the production of lime was on the increase, as an estimate for the building of a further kiln was also requested. John Pike submitted his estimate for the costs of building a new limekiln and repairing the old kiln to the Rt Hon. Lord Rolle on 21 February 1801. Work consisted of digging out the ground for the new kiln which was to measure 24ft sq. A total of 400 perches of brick were needed, which at a cost of 1s.9d. per perch came to a sum of £35. Additional labour incurred costs of £3.3s. All materials were to be paid for by Lord Rolle. A total of 4,500 bricks were required for the building of the new kiln, as well as 4,000 bricks for the old kiln, which must have been undergoing a complete rebuild. Lord Rolle agreed to Pike's estimate.

Accounts books for the Salterton Lime Kilns for the year 1805–06 show a list of customers and the manager's various disbursements. The largest quantity of lime, at 6.s. per hogshead* and ashes at 3s. per hogshead, was purchased by Lord Rolle for the total sum of £197.3s.6d., whilst the lowest quantity was bought by John Warrington of Otterton at the cost of 1s.6d. The limekiln customers, who were probably mainly Rolle Estate tenants, came from East Budleigh, Salterton, Otterton, Kersbrook, Knowle, Venn Ottery, Bicton, Littleham, Tidwell, Withycombe and Topsham. A total of 2,731 hogsheads of lime and 263 hogsheads of ashes were sold to 71 customers, bringing in a revenue of £858.13s.6d. The combined quantity of lime and ashes sold came to 2,994 hogsheads, the equivalent of 746 tons.

According to Wilson, writing in the *Devon Historian*, Lord Rolle's prices were higher than those of other local kilns; exactly why this was the case is difficult to establish. The culm necessary for burning the limestone was brought by sea and as the Budleigh Salterton kilns were close to the shore, Rolle gained some advantage over other lime producers whose kilns were up on cliffs. Rolle was, however, somewhat disadvantaged when it came to the limestone. Whereas other owners had built their kilns close to ready supplies, he had to transport it. It is unlikely that Lord Rolle's hogsheads of lime were more expensive because they were more generous. Whilst the number of bushels (each c.8 gallons) to a hogshead (c.50 gallons) varied from region to region, most kilns tended to use the same measurements as their local competitors. There is however no obvious reason why Rolle's prices were higher than those of his neighbours.

Running Costs

During the period 1805–06, a total of 39 boatloads of stone was used at the Budleigh Salterton kilns. Lord Rolle's stone boat, with John Phillips as master, delivered 23 loads, three loads came in Jackson's

*1 hogshead = c.50 gallons

boat, 11 loads were brought in a boat belonging to Bass and two loads in an unnamed boat. Of these loads 13 were from Babbicombe, one from Torquay, 24 from Berry Head and one from Churston. The money paid for the stone varied, this probably being due to the different sizes of the vessels. Lord Rolle's delivery of limestone cost £6.16s.8d. per boat, whereas Jackson's cost £5.3s.4d., Bass's £3.6s.8d. and the unnamed boat £2.10s.

The amount of fuel required to burn limestone was estimated at ten quarters of culm to one boatload of stones. A total of 360 quarters of culm, which cost on average 14s. per quarter, was purchased at just under £249 for the year 1805/6. As Budleigh Salterton lay within the Port of Exeter, the custom-house there exacted £1 in tax for the culm delivered to the limekiln.

In addition to the cost of limestone and culm, money was also needed for labour (such as loading the kilns and attending to them) and repairs to the kilns or boats and various other equipment. The entries referring to the boats, are mostly due to wear and tear, although in 1805 Lord Rolle paid £17.7s.6d. for a new boat to be built by Thomas Bishop. The boat was then caulked with oakum from Topsham (2s.) and a further quarter hundredweight of white oakum (7s.); the cost of tarring the boat was 4s. In addition to this, the anchor and mooring came to £2.17s.11d.

> **Sample Expenses, June–December 1813**
> The loan of Robert Smith's lighter (boat for transfering goods from ship to wharf) to unload culm – £1
> Repair of the walk used by the horses to bring limestone up from the beach – 15s.
> A boy sent to Bicton to get culm bags – 6d.
> A book for lime burners purchased from the local stationery stores – 6d.
> Rope purchased from Mr Manley of Topsham – £24.10s.3d.
> A shovel purchased from William Webber for the use of the burner – 3s.

Workers and Wages

An account book for the year 1813 shows wages of varying amounts paid to men working at the limekilns. James Western and William Webber were paid 6d. for cleaning ashes from the kilns. Wages paid by John Kay the kiln agent 'on account of landing limestone and culm' to James Western and William Webber amounted to £25. Neither man was able to write, and so simply made his mark after receiving his money.

Grandad Burch with Arthur Skinner, Moor Lane, 1920s.   (KATH GOODING)

In the harvest field, Moor Lane, 1920s. Left to right: Fred Gooding, Herb Yeats, Bill Cann, Joe Pratt, Ted Gooding, George Matthews, Arthur Skinner, Percy Burch, Frank Gooding.   (KATH GOODING)

Western and Webber were also paid for cleaning the kilns and measuring culm, for which they received 6s. and beer to the value of 2s.4d. With the beer given to Western and Webber costing a third of the money given to them, it would seem they were hearty drinkers!

For those working at the Budleigh Salterton limekilns, it was not only thirsty work, but also hungry work. One entry shows lunch consisting of bread and cheese at 1s.11d. followed by three quarts of beer and six of cider (18 pints in all!) at the cost of 5s.9d. For dinner, a leg of mutton at what seems the extraordinary price of 9s.2d., complete with potatoes, dripping and a further helping of bread and cheese costing 4s. was provided. To wash all the food down, beer and cider worth 6d. was provided, which seems a somewhat meagre amount when compared with the liquor enjoyed at lunch-time. Either the men were given food as part of their wages or Lord Rolle was simply a generous employer. Whatever the case, the men ate and drank well in the workplace!

A letter dated 9 April 1815 from Richard Hore of Exmouth to Mr John Daw, Lord Rolle's agent at Bicton, indicates that Lord Rolle was not always generous with his money. Hore, a former employee, wrote that he thought it a 'very great hardship that his Lordship would not pay him two months' wages as it had been such a bad summer'. To consolidate his claim of hardship, he also made it known that he had a large family to support. Hore went on to say that he hoped that his Lordship would take into consideration the fact he had been a servant of his for almost nine years, during which time he had always done Lord Rolle justice. He was, however, no longer able to support his family and, thinking that his Lordship would not be offended, had taken a job as a shipper on someone else's boat. It is not known whether Richard Hore received a reply.

The above account of the limekilns at Budleigh Salterton has been drawn from extant records which cover a short period of time from the late-eighteenth century to the early-nineteenth century, as little else alludes to them. Whilst the limekilns do not appear in White's *Directory of Devon* of 1850, the 1851 Census shows three people who were possibly involved with them. The occupation of William Gore, living at the Granary, was given as lime burner. William Webber, born in 1786 and living in Chapel Street, could be the same William Webber who was paid to clean out ashes from the kiln. Similarly, James Webber, a mariner living in Salterton Hill, could well be the James Webber mentioned above as working at the kilns.

News by Post

One entry in the account books shows that 3s.4d. were paid for five letters from Brixham. At this time the penny post was not yet in place, so any letter being delivered by the postman had to be paid for or it was taken away. As the delivery of a letter meant that the sender was well, it was often assumed that there was no need to read the contents! The postman was therefore often sent on his way, taking the letter with him.

Wind and Weather

A letter dated 3 July 1813 from Christopher Bartlett of Brixham was forwarded to Mr Kay of Budleigh Salterton after a delivery of 152 quarters of culm from Neath was discharged from the *Goodintent*, the master of which was Thomas Petherbridge. Mr Bartlett had the following complaint:

Captain Petherbridge informed me he had very great difficulty in getting your men to procure him that little ballast which he had, and although not more than half so much as he wanted he should not have got that had it not been for his own people. The vessel as it happened got home safe but I assure you had a gale of wind come on from the southward and westward it would have been impossible for her to work home in the light state she was in. If at any time you should want more culm I should be happy to supply it you but it will be necessary the vessel should be discharged and ballasted in one day. The moment Petherbridge arrives home I will make enquiry about the rope you mention and if he has it will take care it shall be sent up to you but I shall be surprised if he has it on board unless it's by mistake or some unavoidable circumstance.

The above letter demonstrates how seafaring vessels were very much at the mercy of the elements. This fact is also reflected in a letter dated 5 December 1813 from William Clarke of Brixham to John King of Budleigh Salterton:

If you are in whant at any time drope mee a line and if wind and weather will permit the [Nutley] to go on that shoar you may have the cargo at one shilling a quarter.

Another letter from Christopher Bartlett, dated 7 December 1813 and addressed to John King, illustrates the effect had by winter weather on the transportation of goods by sea:

Reapers, 1900s. (STEVE RICHARDSON)

Working with the horse and cart, 1900s. (STEVE RICHARDSON)

Harvesting at Budleigh Salterton, 1900s. The gasworks storage container can be seen to the far right of the picture. (STEVE RICHARDSON)

'Paradise Common', Budleigh Salterton, 1900s. (STEVE RICHARDSON)

Percy Burch with Lilly Bastin, Moor Lane, 1920s.   (KATH GOODING)

I am sorry to say its impossible any vessel can come to your place with culm at this season of the year indeed its considered very hazardous even in summer and I would particularly advise you as a friend always in the future to get your stock in the summer months otherwise you will be sure to be disappointed in the winter. In the summer when there is a possibility of coming up I shall be always happy to serve you.

Having passed on this advice Bartlett also confessed, 'I have got the rope, which Captain Petherbridge brought away through mistake and will send it up at the first opportunity'.

Mining Manganese

A lease dated 24 June 1810 indicates that manganese – a metallic element and important component of steels and alloys – was possibly found on Lord Rolle's Estate. The lease granted to John William Williams of Duryard Lodge, Exeter, Nicholas Trebilcock of Budleigh, a miner, and Richard Trelease of Budleigh, also a miner, for a term of 14 years gave them the right to search for manganese on Lord Rolle's land.

With regards to the miners Trebilcock and Trelease, it would appear from their names and occupations that they were Cornishmen, not born and bred in Budleigh. Two and a half years later new parties took over the lease, implying the venture was unsuccessful.

The new lease, dated 31 December 1812, grants James Squire of Newton St Cyres and Zachary Turner of Exeter the licence to dig for manganese on Lord Rolle's Estate in various parishes, including that of East Budleigh, for a term of 21 years.

One specific condition with regard to Budleigh Salterton forbids the opening up of any grounds near the cliffs, without first obtaining Lord Rolle's permission in writing. The lease contained many other stipulations. Any manganese that was found was to be 'raised, pulverised, washed, picked, dressed and made merchantable and fit for sale'. It was then to be carried away, converted and disposed of for the leaseholder's own use. Of course, the manganese came at a price: the lease-holders were to pay either 'one full sixth part of any manganese that may be found' or, 'thirty shillings for every ton of manganese raised' to Lord Rolle. Any manganese for the use of Lord Rolle was to be heaped within 40yds from the spot where it had been found. One day's notice was to be given before weighing the manganese. If 20 tons of manganese was removed without Lord Rolle's knowledge, he would seize the manganese and sell it, with any money raised being used to pay his share and the remaining money going to the leaseholder.

Lord Rolle was also to have access to all account books, letters and papers containing evidence of the quantity of manganese and sale thereof.

The leaseholders were neither permitted to dig within 20ft of any house or building on Lord Rolle's property, nor to wilfully waste, spoil or damage any orchards. If the digging of a particular pit or shaft was to cease for a period of 12 months, all the rubbish taken out was to be thrown back in and a quantity of earth or soil placed over it. All tenants whose property had been damaged by the digging were to be compensated.

As for the carriage of the manganese, should the leaseholders own an insufficient number of horses and carts for this purpose, a proviso was to come into force. They were to employ Lord Rolle's tenants and hire their horses, carts and carriages. For this, the tenants were to receive monetary remuneration, provided, of course, that the tenants 'demean and behave themselves to the satisfaction of James Squire'.

If digging was abandoned or not carried out 'in a proper manner' for a period of six months, the 21-year term would be curtailed. A further condition required Squire to have at least four workmen 'continually digging', or have the lease curtailed.

There is no evidence to indicate whether manganese was found, let alone in sufficient quantities to market. Early maps do not show any indication of old workings or mine shafts, nor does White's *Directory* of 1850 mention any such activity. It can therefore be assumed that if any activity did actually take place, it was probably of an explorative nature only.

References:

A. Born, 'Limestone, Limekilns and the Lime Burning Industry, North and West of Dartmoor', *Transactions of the Devonshire Association* (1991) vol.123.

T.M. Brushfield, *Mate's Illustrated Budleigh Salterton*, (Bournemouth, Mate, 1902).

Devon Record Office: 158M T68; 96M/Box 41/5; 96M/Box 2/12C Lease; 96M/Box 2/12A; 96M add vols. 18/3 Disbursements at Salterton Kilns 1805; 96M/Box 2/16 Lime Burners Book Salterton Kilns; 96M/Box2/12A Letters and various papers; 96M/Box18/10 Lease; 96M add vols. 18/1 Ledger Salterton Kilns.

D. Evans, 'The Technique of Lime Burning', *Devon and Cornwall Notes and Queries* (1987), vol.36, part 1.

R. Polwhele, *The History of Devonshire* (Dorking, Kohler and Coombes, 1977).

R.E. Wilson, 'Lime Burning in East Devon', *Devon Historian* (1980) no.21.

Chapter 6

The Railway Arrives – Late

A letter published in *The Star* 14 September 1892 reads as follows:

One of the prettiest corners of the Rolle Estate is a tiny bay on the South Devon coast that rejoices in the imposing title Budleigh Salterton. It is approached by coach from Exmouth, a distance of six miles and as yet those EVIL GENII the railway contractors and the speculative builder know it not. Though the voice of the tripper is almost unheard on its beach, some interesting people have found their way hither.

This letter was signed Mr & Mrs T. Adolphius Trollope.

Whilst the Trollopes were indeed correct in saying that the railway had not yet reached Budleigh Salterton, their comment about the trippers was not general consensus. Those making a case for a railway line from Exeter to Exmouth were saying that the tripper had reached Budleigh Salterton some 40 years earlier. It was suggested in an entry in Trewman's *Flying Post* of December 1851 that those who travelled to Exmouth and Budleigh Salterton by coach during the summer months were in a position to judge the quantity of day visitors. As proof of the popularity of the two seaside towns, it was stated that a single coach, running to Budleigh and back, had often taken in excess of 100 passengers a day.

Plans and Proposals

The Exeter to Exmouth railway was proposed in 1825 but was not finally completed until 1861. A year later, the Sidmouth Railway and Harbour Bill of 1862 included a line to Budleigh Salterton, whilst the Sidmouth and Budleigh Salterton Act of July 1863 allowed for a line from Tipton St John, but neither of them resulted in the actual building of a line.

In September 1863 the Exeter & Exmouth Railway Company reported at their half-yearly meeting that takings were up compared with 1862. Those who had put money into the company thought this an excellent opportunity to extend the line to Budleigh Salterton, as a means of increasing dividends.

A public meeting was held at the Globe Hotel in Exmouth in January 1865 to discuss whether the building of a railway from the Ottery Road station of the South Western Railway through Budleigh Salterton to Exmouth would be advantageous to the area. Mr Bird, an engineer, explained the route and Dr Land made the case in its favour. Mr Prettejohn declared that such a railway would be prejudicial to the interest of Exmouth. The matter was put to a vote: ten voted for the railway, 13 against.

The Sidmouth Line

The railway came to Sidmouth in July 1874 but by the following month the advantages of this were regarded as questionable. It had apparently brought 'rough types' to the regatta who had, so it was said, 'helped to turn the beautiful esplanade into a minor Bartholemew Fair, with its nut shooting and other stalls and its mountebank dancers'. By September, however, the line was reported as being an 'astonishing success'. The success was, however, not great enough to ensure the emergence of the Budleigh Salterton line, authorised by the Sidmouth Railway Act of August 1876.

The Budleigh Salterton Railway Act

At the Rolle Estate annual manor court, held during October 1881, it was said that the directors of the London & South Western Railway Company had visited Budleigh Salterton and been struck by its attractions as a watering-place. Among the neighbourhood's chief beauties were its hills and valleys, but of course these features also made it difficult to build a railway cheaply. Many other attempts to bring the railway to Budleigh Salterton failed and it was not until 1894 that those wanting a rail link heard good news, with the passing of the Budleigh Salterton Railway Act.

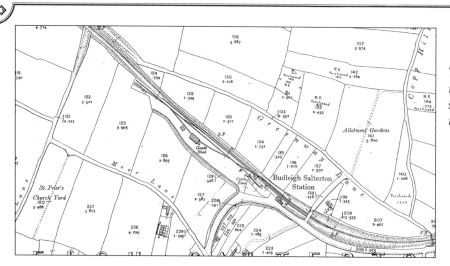

The 1905 Ordnance Survey map (scale: 25in to 1 mile) showing the railway station in open land.
(CLINTON DEVON ESTATES)

'The Salterton lads off to lend a helping hand'. The sailors at Budleigh Salterton railway station during the First World War are thought to be, left to right: *Walter Mears, Rogers, ?, Sedgemoor, Pearcey, Gent Mears, Pearcey, Pearcey.*
(NICK LOMAN COLLECTION)

The 1934 Ordnance Survey map (scale: 25in to 1 mile; reduced) showing the railway station within a built-up area.
(CLINTON DEVON ESTATES)

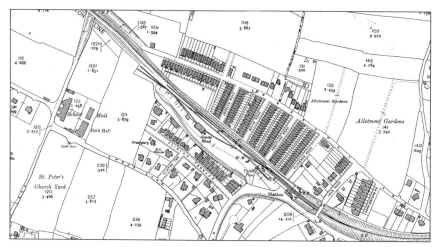

Off to the Army, c.1914.

The Hon. Mark Rolle was on the board and the London & South Western Railway was to work the line. The trustees of the Rolle Estate, over whose land the railway would cross guaranteed the following:

to augment net receipts for up to twenty years after the opening to ensure 3 per cent per annum on called-up capital.

The Exmouth Dock Company was not in favour of the Budleigh Salterton line, as it would affect their trading as a result of which they would lose 25 per cent of their income.

Providing for the Navvies

The *East Budleigh and Budleigh Salterton Parish Magazine* of November 1895 informed its readers that the 'first sod of the new railway' connecting Budleigh Salterton to London was to be cut on 6 November of that year. Shortly after, reported the magazine, around 300 railway workers were to be located at Budleigh Salterton:

popularly known as 'navvies', but the word 'navvy' was in days gone by, and is yet at times, a bye-word of reproach, an unjust and undeserved reproach in those days, as we trust it will be proved to be amongst us in

the next few months. We are in hopes that the contractors, Messrs Aird and Co., who are well known for the kind interest they take in those whom they employ, will build a Mission Room, to be used perhaps also as a Reading Room, amongst the huts in which the workers live, and that a Lay Missionary, with the sanction of the Vicar, will come to live amongst them, and help us to provide for the material, moral, and spiritual welfare of the men. We have no doubt, that with the help of the contractors and of the promoters of the railway, a sufficient sum will be raised locally to pay the Missionary and support the Mission Room, which we hope may prove a centre of good influence amongst the workers, who we must remember are mostly beyond the reach of our ordinary parochial agencies, and exposed to exceptional temptations and hardships. If all will try, as opportunity offers, to take an active interest in the spiritual and social welfare of this large body of guests coming into our parish their stay amongst us will assuredly prove a blessing both to us and them.

In March 1896, £1.16s.7d. (the balance left over from the Navvy Supper Account) and £2.7s. (proceeds from an entertainment at the Public Rooms), were put in a Navvy Missionary Fund. This was to provide for the salary of a lay missionary. It was also said that other donations made to the vicar for the fund would be gratefully received.

The Building of the Line

On Wednesday 6 November 1895 Budleigh Salterton was festooned with flags. By noon people had made their way to Mr Bickley's field in Greenway Lane to watch Lady Gertrude Rolle cut the first sod for the long-awaited railway line from Tipton to Budleigh Salterton. There were loud cheers as she placed the sod in a silver-mounted oak wheelbarrow, using a silver spade with an ebony handle.

To celebrate the occasion, a public luncheon was held. The speeches made were naturally very positive about the forthcoming railway, stressing the advantages it would bring to the community of Budleigh Salterton. In the evening a public tea, followed by entertainment, was attended by a large crowd.

The line was constructed by Lucas & Aird in a most professional manner, and was completed in about 19 months, six months ahead of time. The new line commenced close to Tipton station and ran along the valley of the Otter to Budleigh Salterton. When travelling along the line from Tipton, sitting on the train facing in the direction of Salterton, passengers passed Harpford (on the left), followed by Newton Poppleford (on the right) and Colaton Raleigh (also on the right). The train then arrived at Budleigh station, with Otterton situated a mere 'gunshot away on the left', whereas East Budleigh village was a mile away. One would have thought that naming the station 'Budleigh' and not 'Otterton', could have confused many travellers unacquainted with the district, causing them to believe they had already reached Budleigh Salterton.

Despite its size Budleigh station was awarded a stationmaster, possibly due to the fact that Lord Rolle lived nearby, at Bicton. It was perhaps thought to be appropriate to have a stationmaster present at the local station of a director of the London & South Western Railway Company.

Budleigh station was comprised of a private office, a combined booking-office and waiting-room with table and seats, a ladies' room with table and chairs, the floor of which was laid with linoleum, a porters' room, a small goods shed and an ample yard. The stationmaster resided in a house a little distance from the station.

Continuing the journey from Budleigh station towards Budleigh Salterton, East Budleigh village was passed on the right. The approach to Budleigh Salterton rose from 1:100ft to 1:50ft. On the left, there was a view of the sea. Budleigh Salterton was finally reached through a substantial cutting over the last quarter mile of the line.

The station itself was similar to that at Budleigh, but somewhat more extensive. The stationmaster was Mr T. Russell, a native of Exeter, for whom a house had been built overlooking the station. The yard consisted of an engine-house, goods office, water tank and a shed which trucks could enter at one end and exit at the other. A short piece of new road served the station from the town, along which it was anticipated that building would sooner or later commence.

The entire length of the line was 6 miles and 33 chains. No engineering difficulties had been encountered whilst building the line, although one of the temporary bridges erected by the line contractors had been washed away during the winter of 1895–96 when the Otter overflowed its banks. Three iron-girder bridges carried the line across the Otter, four overhead bridges carried roads over the line, and between Stoneborough and Budleigh Salterton there was a wooden footbridge. The places served by the Budleigh station were Otterton, East Budleigh, Bicton, Yettington, Colaton Raleigh, Hawkerland and Kingston. The Budleigh Salterton station served Budleigh Salterton, Knowle and Kersbrook.

Knowle House, 1950s.   (STEVE RICHARDSON)

The Opening Ceremony

The ceremonial opening of the line took place on 14 May 1897. Officials from the London & South Western Railway Company who had travelled from Waterloo boarded a special train at Sidmouth Junction. Just after midday they travelled with other passengers to the station at Tipton St John which had been decorated for the occasion. They were greeted by children singing the National Anthem, under the direction of the schoolmaster.

The wife of the Budleigh Salterton Railway Company's chairman, Mrs Hugh Williams-Drummond, drove the train from Tipton St John, its engine decorated with flags, foliage, and her own portrait. Upon arrival at its destination the train was welcomed by inhabitants of Budleigh Salterton and the surrounding area, as well as the music of the Sidmouth Volunteers' Band.

Southern Engine at Budleigh Salterton railway station, 1950s. (NICK LOMAN COLLECTION)

'Budleigh Salterton' No. 21C144 Southern Railway West Country Class Pacific 4-6-2 Engine, 1945. (NICK LOMAN COLLECTION)

Station Road in the early-twentieth century. (STEVE RICHARDSON)

The Green, 1950s. (STEVE RICHARDSON)

This footbridge served as a right of way to Knowle House, which the people pictured here in c.1910 may have occupied. The brick pillars are all that remain of this bridge in 2005, whilst the view gained in this photograph is totally obscured by trees. (STEVE RICHARDSON)

The Railway Comes to Budleigh Salterton

'The Railway Comes To Budleigh Salterton', to the tune 'We'll all go a-hunting today', was written for the opening of the Budleigh Salterton railway station, 14 May 1897.

What a grand holiday
Was the fourteenth of May,
When the first Train to Salterton came;
With what pleasure and pride
To the Station we hied,
To greet it with loudest acclaim.
See hundreds are now on their way,
All bound for the Station are they;
While they sing this glad song
'And now WE shan't be long,
For the Line will be opened today.'

(Chorus) Yes, the Line will be Opened today,
For the first Train is now on its way;
And its passengers bring
The glad tidings they sing –
'The Line will be opened today.'

At the Station we wait,
The excitement is great –
By the clock it is twenty past one,
Then we know the Train's near,
Detonators we hear,
Which rattle away like a gun.
Then into the Station it glides,
'Tis a lady its movement guides:
And we cheer with our might,
As the party alight,
And the Band plays a welcome besides.

(Chorus) The Band plays a welcome refrain
As the passengers leave the first Train,
We had doubted for years,

Now goodbye our fears,
They never will daunt us again.

Now I said to my wife
The next day:– 'On my life,
Trade is bad and Rent's due, as you say,
But I don't care a fig, –
In our best Sunday rig
We'll both go to Tipton today!'

(Chorus) We'll both go to Tipton today,
From Salterton by the Railway:–
'Then,' said she, with a smile,
'We shan't be a great while
Before we're at Tipton today.'

Then Success to the Rail,
And may it never fail
To have passengers forward and back;
And our smart little Town
May prosperity crown
Brought over the new Railway Track.
Long life to the giver so free –
The Lord of the Manor 'tis he –
In my song I would fain
Thank the Donor again,
For his goodness most grateful are we.

(Chorus) For his goodness most grateful are we,
No grander gift ever could be;
And with truth we can say,
'Twas a red letter day
For Salterton down by the Sea.

After the line had been declared open by Mrs Williams-Drummond, her husband handed it over to Wyndham Portal, chairman of the London & South Western Railway Company. Speeches preceded a luncheon, after which most guests departed. Budleigh Salterton people though, continued to celebrate amidst the decorations and inscribed arches.

Service began the very next day, on 15 May 1897, and consisted of eight weekday trains in both directions.

The Link from Budleigh Salterton to Exmouth

The line linking Budleigh Salterton to Exmouth was first proposed by the Rolle trustees in November 1896, but nothing was agreed until June 1898. The following month, the London & South Western Railway Company took control. Those who had supported the building of this line back in 1851 – if indeed they were still around – now saw their forward thinking come to fruition.

When work commenced on the line it was reported in the *South Western Gazette* that:

No Royal Presence, no Duke or Duchess with silver spade, no Director, not even an officer of the company, but only an office boy out of bounds witnessed the cutting of the first sod on one of the prettiest five miles of railway in the sunny south.

The line, 4 miles and 46.3 chains in length, involved a lot of constructional work. Cuttings and embankments involved a vast amount of soil moving and several bridges were erected. From Exmouth, a 3-mile length of the single track traversed a gradient of 1:50ft after going over a 30ft high brick viaduct that was almost a quarter of a mile in length. With the line going over Rolle property came a proviso from the Rolle trustees: they required an intermediate station at Littleham.

On 1 June 1903, a Whit Monday, the line was opened amongst much rejoicing. The first train left Exmouth at 10.30a.m. for Budleigh Salterton and returned at midday, in time for a luncheon and sports.

The End of the Line

Dr Beeching, on being appointed chairman of the British Transport Commission by the Tory government in 1961, produced a report in March 1963 identifying unprofitable activities on the railway. A legacy stemming from Beeching's report was the end

'Navvies' working on the Budleigh Salterton to Exmouth railway line, c.1900. The photograph includes: *Tom Vincent* (back row, second from left) *and Bill Gooding* (middle row, second from left). (STEVE RICHARDSON)

of the line for Budleigh Salterton in March 1967, by which time many other lines had been closed and Beeching had become known as the 'railway axe man'. A legacy of the Exmouth to Budleigh Salterton line remains: the old trackway has now become a popular route for cyclists and walkers.

W.G. Clarke, author of *Oh, Mr Porter!* tells an interesting story concerning Budleigh Salterton station. According to local hearsay, in order to keep Budleigh Salterton exclusive, Lord Clinton used his capacity as a director of the railway company to reject proposals regarding the promotion of Budleigh Salterton. Clarke states that in over 46 years of railway service, he never once saw a poster advertising Budleigh Salterton. Perhaps someone can prove him wrong!

Whilst Clarke's view on poster advertising may be correct, it is not true to say the railway never promoted Budleigh Salterton. A Great Western Railway 1928 publication entitled *Glorious Devon* contains a view of The Promenade and describes Budleigh Salterton as 'a quiet jolly seaside town'.

Budleigh Salterton also gains a mention in the GWR 1926 publication *Devon, The Shire of the Sea Kings*.

References:

East Budleigh and Budleigh Salterton Parish Magzine (various issues dating from 1874–1892).

E.A.G. Clark, *The Ports of the Exe Estuary 1660–1860*, (Exeter, The University of Exeter, 1960).

W.G. Clarke, *Oh, Mr Porter! Life on a Devon Branch Line in the Days of Steam* (Budleigh Salterton, Granary Press, 1983).

B. Davies and J. Evans (eds.), *Budleigh Salterton Past and Present: Collections and Recollections* (photocopy of MS, 1960?), Westcountry Studies Library.

GWR publication, *Devon, The Shire of the Sea Kings* (London, Great Western Railway Company, 1926).

S.P.B. Mais, *Glorious Devon* (London, Great Western Railway Company, 1928).

Westcountry Studies Library: newspaper cuttings.

R.A. Williams, *The London & South-Western Railway: Growth and Consolidation* (Newton Abbot, David & Charles, 1973) vol.2.

Trees cleared at Knowle Hill for the Budleigh Salterton to Exmouth railway line, c.1900.   (STEVE RICHARDSON)

◇

Chapter 7

The Cottage Hospital

The Cottage Hospital, 1920s.

The Infancy Years

The Cottage Hospital, Budleigh Salterton's memorial to Queen Victoria's golden jubilee, was opened for patients on 1 January 1889. Plans for the hospital were first conceived two years earlier, in 1887.

Laying the Foundation-Stone

The foundation-stone was laid on Thursday 8 March 1888 and although the weather was not conducive for the ceremony, a large number of people gathered to witness the occasion. Dr Brushfield gave an opening address that was followed by a short service taken by the vicar. The surpliced choir from Rolle chapel led the hymn singing.

The foundation-stone, a block of Devonshire granite, carries the following inscription: 'This Stone was laid by the Rev. James Boucher, M.A., March 8th, 1888. R.M. Fulford, Architect. J.C. Palmer, Builder.' The munificent

Revd Boucher gave £525 towards the building costs, whilst the Hon. Mark Rolle donated the land on which the hospital was built. Dr Walker proposed a vote of thanks to Lord Rolle, the subscribers, as well as to Revd Boucher for laying the stone.

The Revd Boucher thanked the assemblage but before they all went their own way, he begged them to help maintain the hospital, to ensure it would benefit the neighbourhood for years to come. The crowd responded with three hearty cheers.

Fund-Raising

Lady Gertude Rolle opened a two-day bazaar, held on 22 and 23 August 1888, to raise money for the furnishing of the hospital. Marquees were crammed with manifold stalls laden with both 'fancy and useful articles' that sold readily, with little stock remaining at the end of the two days. All remaining items were to be sold at the opening of the hospital.

Music was provided by the Exmouth Brass Band for the full two days.

In addition to the bazaar Dr Brushfield provided entertainment in the form of 'Two Hour's Illusions', held at the Public Rooms on the evenings of 24 and 25 August. An exhibition of various works of art was also set up by Mr Theobald but unfortunately failed to attract a great number of visitors. These three events raised a combined total of just under £230 for the hospital fund.

Board and Committee Members

The following people were appointed to perform the duties relevant to their assigned roles: the Hon. Mark Rolle (president); Revd Boucher (vice-president); Lady Gertrude Rolle (president of the visiting committee); Messrs R. Walker and T. Evans (medical officers); Mrs Warington (honorary matron); Mr C. Wilson (treasurer); Mr Friend (honorary secretary). A committee was also established and comprised Dr Brushfield (chairman), Mr Bennett, Mr Bourne, Revd Cork, Mr Gush, Revd Harrison, Lt Col Lee, Mrs Lipscombe, Mr Perriam (vicar), Mrs Brushfield, Mrs Romaine, Mrs Callender, Mrs Dryden, Mrs Edwards and Miss Gibbons.

Dr Tom Evans and Mrs Evans at the Red Cross fête, 1951.
(KATH GOODING)

Rules and Regulations

As with all institutions, manifold rules and regulations were formulated. These stipulated that Budleigh Salterton Cottage Hospital was intended for the benefit of poor persons in the Parish of East Budleigh, suffering from accidents or non-infectious diseases that could not be attended to in their own homes. Cases of advanced consumption or 'hopeless' disease would not be received and neither would children under the age of four years, unless attended by their mother.

Those people who had given a total sum of £5 or those giving at least 5s. per annum were entitled to vote at annual meetings. The ladies on the general committee were to form a visiting committee to direct domestic arrangements. A matron was to be appointed and discharged by the committee. She was to report to the medical officers with regard to the treatment of patients, and to the visiting committee with regard to the general order of the hospital and all the stock held in the stores in her charge.

Patients were required to pay 2s.6d. or more in advance, according to their financial status, whilst the medical officers and a lady from the visiting committee were to fix the final payment. The committee would have the power to remit fees. Subscribers of 10s.6d. and multiples thereof, could recommend one patient yearly for each 10s.6d. paid. Each subscriber paying one guinea annually would become a governor, whilst those donating ten guineas would become life governors. Clergymen donating collections would be able to recommend one patient for each half guinea. Only in cases of emergency were patients to be admitted without having had a form of recommendation completed by a subscriber.

Each medical officer was to attend the hospital for a week in succession, although they all had the right to continue the treatment of any patient previously in their care. As there were no medical officers in full attendance at the hospital, emergency cases were to be dealt with by the first medical officer to arrive, but would then be handed over to the appropriate medical officer. No patient was to remain in hospital for more than six weeks unless the matter was approved by the committee; in such cases an increased rate would be charged if necessary. Medical officers were to give their services free of charge, but those patients that were in a position to pay their medical attendant, in addition to the hospital fee, were to do so.

The regulations also stated that all essentials would be provided by the hospital, except for personal clothing and the laundering of the same. Nothing was to be given to patients from any source outside the hospital without first being sanctioned by a medical officer. All drugs and appliances for a patient's use were to come out of hospital funds.

Patients could be discharged from the hospital for misconduct or for neglecting or refusing to obey hospital rules. Whilst in hospital they were to be allowed access to a religious group of their own choosing.

Nursing staff and patients, 1950s. Left to right, back row: *Matron Timporily, Minnie Prout, Mrs Hexter, Kathleen Deller, Mabel Prouse, Lillian Reynolds, ?, ?, Mrs Coles, ?;* front row: *?, ?, Mr Earnshaw, Agnes Gooding, Dorothy Curry, Joan Vinnicombe.* (WENDY MORRISH)

Children's party in the hospital, 1950s. The photograph includes: *Carol Reynolds* (second from right at the back), *Wendy Vinnicombe* (to Carol's right), *Miss Tuke* (in the peaked hat) *and Mrs Hopkins* (in the chair on the left). (WENDY MORRISH)

Hospital staff carnival float 'The National Elf Service', 1980s. Left to right: ? Gillard, Carol ?, Glinnis Heyde, Wendy Morrish, Dr Evans, Joyce Brown. (WENDY MORRISH)

Hospital staff, 1992. Left to right, back row: Gerry Bassett, Dr Evans, Jackie Nelson; front row: Helen Taylor, Wendy Morrish. (WENDY MORRISH)

Left: *Centenary Year. Left to right: Olive Irvine, Dr Evans, Wendy Morrish, Helen Taylor.*
(WENDY MORRISH)

Below: *Budleigh Salterton hospital, 1990s.*
(WENDY MORRISH)

Visitors were permitted, but were to observe the visiting regulations. A visitor's book, open at all times for inspection, was to be kept in the hospital for visitors to comment in. A complaint book was also to be maintained but the committee would not entertain any complaint that was not signed by the complainant.

An annual report with a monetary account was to be published and on reading the hospital's first annual report we find the committee lauding the 'usefulness of the Institution and its benefit to those persons for whom it was principally intended'.

Donations and Subscriptions

Throughout the hospital's first year, many donations were made, such as furniture, books, pictures, games, fruit and vegetables. Mrs George Warington had even donated her services as matron free of charge.

It was stressed that if the hospital was to continue it was most important that the annual subscriptions should not decrease. The residents of neighbouring parishes were also urged to contribute, implying that patients from those parishes had also been admitted to the hospital.

Annual Report, 1889

On 31 December 1889 the building fund showed a deficit of just under £63. This was due to extra work which had been carried out to the sum of just under £81. The maintenance and furnishing account, however, showed a balance in hand of just under £152. In addition to this, just under £1,156 had been invested in the endowment and investment account.

By the end of the hospital's first year in operation, a total of 39 patients had been treated. There had never been a day without patients. On an average day, four patients were in the hospital, remaining there for an average of 40 days.

Annual Report, 1890

In the annual report for the hospital's second year, 1890, the committee stated that the statistics:

demonstrated that the need of such an institution in our midst is clearly proved, and the unabated and increased interest taken in its welfare by all classes is most encouraging and hopeful for the future.

The number of patients treated had risen to 53, compared with 39 during the previous year. At times all of the beds had been occupied, with further people waiting to be admitted.

Although finances were satisfactory, money from subscriptions and offertories had decreased when compared to the previous year. The increase in the number of patients had resulted in higher maintenance fees and the need for nurses (not to mention their wages) but with the extra amount of patients' fees received and the matron's careful handling of the internal economy, funds in hand were £18 higher than the previous year. The building fund deficit had dropped to just over £32, thanks to the generosity of two donors

At the end of this year, plans were afoot to extend the hospital, by means of a bathroom and additional accommodation for the increasing number of patients. Better arrangements were also to be made for the treatment of so-called 'special cases' and improved facilities for resident staff were also in the offing. Donations had already been secured to finance the proposed work.

Dr Walker, who had been concerned with the hospital since its advent, had resigned from his position as a medical officer, but remained one of the 'Honorary Consulting Physicians to the Hospital'.

In addition to her nursing duties at the hospital, Miss Gibbons was appointed to the role of parish nurse. She would not attend those needing treatment in the Cottage Hospital, but would be pleased to call on the sick and lying-in cases amongst the poor of the parish. She would not charge for her attendance but if anyone were in the position to pay for her skills they should do so according to their means. She would however, give half of the payment to the Cottage Hospital and the remaining money to charity. Miss Gibbon would reserve the right to refuse to attend to prospective patients as and when appropriate.

Annual Report, 1891

By the end of the hospital's third year in operation, the number of patients admitted had increased by only one. A total of 31 patients had been deemed 'cured' and discharged, 11 had 'benefited' from their treatment, one had died, and eight remained in the hospital.

As in the previous year, the sum of annual subscriptions and offertories had decreased, but fees paid by patients more than compensated for this. Finally, the deficit of just under £33 in the building fund had been paid off. This was partly due to a handsome donation from the proceeds of local amateur dramatic productions and other offerings. However, in order to clear the debt completely, £10.4s.2d. was transferred from the furnishing fund.

Work to enlarge the hospital had been carried out by J.C. Palmer, and as a result the hospital had gained a bathroom, storeroom, separation ward with cellar, and a dormitory. There had also been alterations to the staircase. Despite having received many generous donations, the hospital still needed a further £100 to cover the cost of the work.

Annual Report, 1892

In the fourth annual report it was stated that 52 patients had been treated during the year 1892, bringing the total number of cases to 192. The finances were described as 'satisfactory', but as during the past two years, subscriptions had not provided the level of income that the hospital required. The money paid by patients had dramatically increased, owing to 'one or two exceptional cases'. A legacy of £450 left to the hospital by a Mrs Palmer had been invested in 'India 3 per cent stock'. Revd Boucher's gift of £1,000 invested in a similar manner had made nearly £485.

Improvements made to the hospital during this year included the addition of a bath with fittings, a large water tank, as well as a new staircase. The old staircase had apparently been rather narrow and steep, making it difficult to carry patients up and down safely. The hospital had been decorated both inside and out.

Due to a serious illness, Miss Gibbons, the parish nurse, had not been able to carry out her work since early in the year. It was not known whether she would take up her duties again.

Annual Report, 1893

According to the annual report of 1893, the number of patients treated during that year dropped to 45. The subscriptions and donations, however, had increased. The hospital's running costs for the year (covering staff, maintenance and treatment of patients) amounted to £190.6s.9d., the weekly average working out at just under £3.15s.

Annual Report, 1894

In 1894 Revd Boucher donated a further £500 which was also put into 'India 3 per cent stock', forming the 'Needy Patients and Surgical Aid Fund'. This fund not only assisted poorer patients with the payment of hospital fees, but also supplied money for surgical appliances.

Once again subscribers were reminded that the matron gave her services freely. Had she demanded a salary, the annual balance would have appeared rather less healthy.

Annual Report, 1895

In the annual report of 1895, the 'Needy Patients and Surgical Aid Fund' was deemed 'a great blessing to many'. The interest from the fund had been used to pay hospital costs for those who could not otherwise have afforded to stay at the hospital. The fund had

also supplied 'various surgical and nursing necessaries' for the treatment of such patients.

The report also referred to the construction of the railway. Far from greeting this development with enthusiasm, the committee feared that:

owing to the construction of the railway, and the possibility of accidents or sickness occurring amongst those engaged on the work, the resources of the Hospital may be tried to a greater extent than heretofore, and consequently increased expenditure may have to be incurred.

Annual Report, 1896

Revd Boucher gave another £500 in 1896 and, once again, this was invested in 'India 3 per cent stock'. The committee stressed that the need for such donations was reflected in the high number of applicants to the Needy Patients and Surgical Aid Fund

Despite the committee's fears about the construction of the railway and a possible strain on hospital resources, no financial loss seems to have been incurred. Five workers had been treated at the hospital, two of whom had died. The contractor of the line, John Aird MP, paid the mens' hospital fees. It would appear that he held the hospital in high esteem, as he also donated a further £5.5s. to the establishment.

Celebrating the Diamond Jubilee

In the annual report of 1896, the committee also refers to Queen Victoria's diamond jubilee which was to take place the following year. To commemorate this occasion, the committee thought it appropriate to make some improvements to the hospital.

Your Committee would remind the inhabitants of Salterton and the surrounding districts that this year will form an epoch in the history of this Empire, as, should our beloved Queen be spared to the 20ᵗʰ June next, she will have completed 60 years reign over these realms. Inasmuch as our Cottage hospital is a [golden] jubilee memorial, it surely would be a fitting tribute of our gratitude and loyalty, if one and all were to combine to crown that memorial by contributing towards making it what it ought to be, a Model Cottage Hospital. A cottage for a man and his wife, with a laundry attached, and the erection of a decent mortuary chamber, are very much needed. Towards the latter about £150 is to be handed to the Committee, being the balance of the purchase money of the Coffee tavern. This is in accordance with the wish of the original donor of that Institution [Revd James Boucher], and is only another proof of how great is his desire that the Hospital, for which he has already done so much, should be made as complete as possible.

Hospital staff Christmas dinner, 1960s. Left to right: *Mabel Prouse, Minnie Prout, Joan Vinnicombe, ?, Mrs Squires?, Dr Squires, Joyce Brown.*

(WENDY MORRISH)

Hospital staff Christmas fancy-dress party, 1960s. Left to right, standing: *Joan Vinnicombe, Lavender Plant, ?, ?, Joyce Brown, Mrs Hexter, ?, Lillian Reynolds, Mrs Partridge, Mrs Osbourne, Miss Tuke;* kneeling: *Laura Vincent, Sister Morris.*

(WENDY MORRISH)

Hospital staff Christmas dinner, 1960s. Left to right, standing: *Miss Tuke, Sister Morris, ?, Jennifer Shipton, Agnes Gooding, Margaret Strawbridge, Mrs Partridge, Brian Hopkins, ?, Margaret Snell, Joyce Brown, Mr Hopkins, Lillian Reynolds, Poppy Scott;* sitting: *Mrs Hexter, Joan Vinnicombe, Dorothy Curry, Mabel Prouse, Minnie Prout, Laura Vincent, Mrs Osbourne.*

(WENDY MORRISH)

At the suggestion of the matron the hospital provided entertainment for all the patients, as part of the diamond jubilee celebrations. A large number of the patients' friends were invited to share the occasion and they brought food with them, such as strawberries and cream. Children danced around a maypole on the lawn and in the evening it was the adults' turn to dance. The event closed with the matron being given three cheers, followed by a rendering of God Save the Queen and three cheers for Her Majesty.

Annual Report, 1897

During the course of 1897, a detached cottage was constructed for a resident man and his wife. A laundry and mortuary were also completed. Lord Rolle had provided the land upon which the new buildings were erected. The work was financed through a house-to-house collection in Salterton which had acquired a sum of just over £215, which was added to the hosptial's available funds of £160. A further £125 was, however, still needed to cover the cost of the work and the committee wished the new facilities to 'be opened free of debt'. They therefore appealed to all those in the surrounding district who had benefitted from the hospital facilities to contribute.

The number of patients treated in 1897 fell to 41, thus the sum of patients' fees also fell, but subscriptions and offertories remained at the level of the previous year.

The Hospital's Tenth Year

In April 1899 it was announced that the hospital needed a piano to 'brighten and cheer the monotonous lives of the patients'. There was already a piano in the hospital at that time, but it belonged to the matron, Mrs Warington. It would therefore seem that the matron was leaving the hospital and taking her piano with her. There was also a request for 12 new bibles.

In the tenth annual report the committee recounted how the hospital had developed since its early days. The hospital had progressed from having one female and one male ward, each with three beds, to becoming 'nearly a model of what a Cottage Hospital should be'. During the hospital's first decade a grand total of 446 patients had been treated.

The committee also gave details of the resignation of the matron, Mrs Warington, the loss of whom was to be:

most keenly felt, not only by the Committee, but by the community at large. By her devotion and zeal, by her loving and tender care of the patients, by her deep

religious tone, and her entire disregard of self in the performances of her onerous and often sad duties, she has endeared herself to all, and will leave behind a name that will ever be remembered with gratitude, and one that will never be forgotten by the inhabitants of Salterton.

Along with the matron's resignation came that of the committee chairman, Dr Brushfield, due to ill health. As one of those who had originally advocated the founding of a cottage hospital, he had been involved with the hospital from its opening.

Finally, the committee proffered 'best thanks' to:

the gentleman of the Medical staff, to the Hon Secretary and Treasurer, and to all those who, by their contributions and presents, have assisted in maintaining the usefulness of the Institution, and have helped to further the good work that is being carried on.

The Modern-Day Hospital

The Cottage Hospital has continued to serve those in need of medical attention throughout the years. Staff ensured the hospital was a cheerful place, especially at Christmas, when it was festooned with decorations and fancy-dress parties were organised for patients and staff alike.

The year of 2004 saw the closure of Budleigh Salterton hospital for refurbishment. It is due to reopen in 2005, with a new specialist stroke unit.

References:
East Budleigh and Budleigh Salterton Parish Magazine (issues dating from the period 1888–1899).

Christmas decorations at the hospital, 1960s.

(WENDY MORRISH)

Chapter 8

Religion

Church Attendance – The Early Years

Prior to Budleigh Salterton having its own religious houses, local inhabitants either attended All Saints' Church at East Budleigh or the Church of St Margaret and St Andrew at Littleham. As the crow flies, the distance to either church from the High Street traffic lights in Budleigh Salterton is about 2 miles. The churchgoer's choice of church could therefore have been influenced by whether he or she lived on one side of Budleigh Salterton, or the other.

The building of the chapel of ease in Budleigh Salterton in 1813 doubtless made life much easier for the inhabitants. This was, however, not the first religious building in Budleigh Salterton; the Wesleyans were one step ahead of their Church of England counterparts – their chapel was built in 1812.

The interior of the Methodist Church, 1950s.
(METHODIST CHURCH ARCHIVE)

The Wesleyan Chapel

A London bookseller, James Lackington, who had settled at Budleigh Salterton due to ill health, erected the Wesleyan chapel in 1812 at the cost of £1,700. Walton, writing in the *Wesley Historical Society Proceedings* (1928), believed that Lackington's generosity stemmed from the fact that the people of his newly adopted parish were languishing in 'spiritual destitution and darkness'. Walton also informs us that the local landowner, Lord Rolle, was considered 'a bigoted Churchman', which meant that Lackington had to act with great circumspection when purchasing a piece of land on which to build his church. It was not until he had acquired a freehold property with a large garden, called Ash Villa, over which Lord Rolle had no control, that Lackington announced his intentions of building a Methodist church. He encountered bitter opposition; none of the Rolle Estate tenants were permitted to help him. As a result he had to employ a builder from Exeter and import building materials from outside the area. Lackington remained undeterred, apparently insisting that 'If the chapel has to be built of golden sovereigns, it will be built.' When the Methodist church finally opened in 1813, it was named 'The Temple'.

Lackington secured the services of the Revd John Hawtry who, according to Walton, was described as 'an able, zealous, good man' who had managed to

James Lackington's resting-place, East Budleigh churchyard.
(AUTHOR)

Holy Trinity, a chapel of ease, West Terrace, 1900s.
(STEVE RICHARDSON)

The Wesleyan Methodist church, known as 'The Temple', pictured during the first decade of the twentieth century. (STEVE RICHARDSON)

The Revd J. Penrose Hodgson, minister of the Methodist church, 1921–28.
(METHODIST CHURCH ARCHIVE)

Impression of the Methodist church intended to replace the original James Lackington building in 1904.
(METHODIST CHURCH ARCHIVE)

Entrance to the Methodist church with the Old Manse to the left, 1890s.
(METHODIST CHURCH ARCHIVE)

Revd George Allen and Granfer Watts, 1934.
(METHODIST CHURCH ARCHIVE)

convert many 'prominent Church of England people'. In 1815, just two years after The Temple was opened, Lackington died. Some 25 years later his widow proposed selling The Temple, but she was persuaded to transfer the title of the chapel to the Superintendent of the Exeter Circuit and other trustees for 10s.

The building was altered and enlarged on various occasions. In 1904 a new building replaced the old one at a cost of £5,500. The new chapel, also called The Temple, underwent alterations in 2004, in order to improve access for those with physical disabilities.

The Chapel of Ease

Holy Trinity, a chapel of ease, also known as the Rolle Chapel, was built in 1813 near the junction of East and West Terrace at the cost of about £900 by Lord Rolle, in retaliation, so it was said, to the building of the Methodist church. It was enlarged in 1837 at a further cost of £1,100. Although the chapel had cost £2,000 in total, it was still regarded as being unworthy of Budleigh Salterton. Moreover, it was never consecrated.

James Davidson, a man interested in Devon's history, visited many Devon churches during the nineteenth century. Having visited Budleigh Salterton on 14 July 1840, he described the chapel of ease as follows:

The building consists of an open area of 3 aisles with large and deep galleries one of which contains\ an organ. The windows are underpointed arches and are formed into lancet lights and there are crosses on the exterior gables but the structure though recent has no pretensions to architectural beauty. The only monumental notices are as follows.

Tablet: Emilia daughter of John Halsy esq. – wife of William Dunsford esq. Died 14 September 1829 aged 46 years – Erected by her sister Maria Elizabeth Budden.

Tablet: Maria Elizabeth daughter of John Halsey esq. relict of Major Richard Budden of the East India Company's Service. Died 26 April 1832 aged 51. Erected by her children.

Tablet: Marcia Elizabeth second daughter of Major Budden Hon. East India Company's Service and Maria Elizabeth his wife. Died 29 December 1832 aged 21. Erected by her two sisters.

Davidson's comment on the chapel's lack of architectural beauty possibly explains why it was regarded in certain circles as being unworthy of Budleigh Salterton. Beatrix Cresswell, who had visited many Devon churches during the period 1902–13, was of the same opinion as Davidson. Writing in 1920 she insisted that the building 'had no architectural merits' and that 'it might be described as having no architecture at all'.

The chapel of ease contained box pews. In 1887 it was announced that the sides and ends of the pews were to be lowered, and the doors removed. The reasons behind these alterations were given as making the seats more comfortable and precluding the noise of doors opening and closing. It would appear, however, that the real reason behind the intended modifications was the 'unseemly behaviour' which occurred:

in some of the pews under shelter of their high walls to the intense annoyance of the congregation, and to the dishonour of God.

By modifying the box pews it was hoped that the 'evil deeds' would 'shrink in very shame from the light to which they will be now exposed'.

As can still be seen in some churches, the congregation was seated, according to family or estate, in 'high deal' (i.e. with a high back, sides and a door) pews or seats. These seats were often a cause of great friction between certain church-goers. Individual families of the parish petitioned the bishop of the diocese for the permission to erect a seat for their estate, and upon sanction being given, the seat was then built and maintained by the family.

One may wonder just how high the seats in Rolle Chapel were. It is possible that they were of a similar height to those in Staverton church. These seats were often subject to ridicule, a fact which is evident in the following lines:

Here Squier [sic] came and sat the service through,
And Squier's lady, sons and daughters too,
And Squier's friends and sometimes his relations,
And Squier's staff (according to their stations);
I've heard it said the Squier felt remorse
That he was not allowed to bring his horse;
So dark and stable-like was Squier's pew
That maybe Squier did – and no one knew?

After the modifications, all seats in Rolle Chapel became accessible to both rich and poor. As a concession to those who had formerly rented their own pews, they were allowed to claim one seat (not one pew) until the organ voluntary commenced, after which time anyone could take an empty seat and did not have to move from it.

An appeal was made in 1888 for extra money towards the cost of maintaining services provided by the chapel, which amounted to £5 per week. The offertories averaged £2.10s. per week and covered ordinary expenses, but extra money was needed for the Poor Fund, the Sunday school and other outgoings. The vicar saw no alternative but to ask those who valued the services to contribute towards their maintenance.

The Building of St Peter's Church

In c.1890 the Hon. Mark Rolle offered to provide a site for a new church to replace the chapel of ease, as well as offering to build the replacement. Both offers were accepted and on Tuesday 24 November 1891, a fine sunny day, Miss Rolle laid the foundation-stone of St Peter's Church.

Revd Smith's farewell, 1960. Left to right, back row: *Phyllis Trick, Amy Trick, Maurice Trick, Fred Lovesey* (in glasses), *Jeff Carter;* middle row: *Mrs Southball, Sally Pope, Dorothy Smith, Frizzey Jewell, Revd Smith, Edith Lovesey, ?, Ethel Bond, Nellie Jewell;* front row: *Miss Grovenor, ?, Mrs Sage, Mrs Benoke, Robert Bond, Sue Bond, Mrs Vinnicombe.*

(METHODIST CHURCH ARCHIVE)

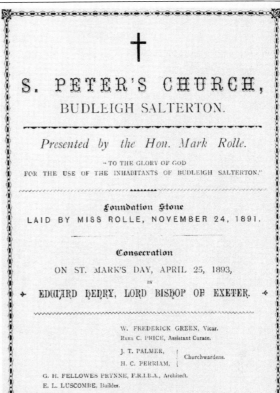

An artistic impression of St Peter's Church, showing the intended tower and the front cover of the consecration service sheet. (ST PETER'S CHURCH)

Above left: *St Peter's Church from the south-west, 1950s.* (STEVE RICHARDSON)

Above: *St Peter's Church (with original furnishings), 1950s.* (STEVE RICHARDSON)

Left: *The 'children's corner' of St Peter's Church was dedicated in 1935.* (STEVE RICHARDSON)

A very large number of people were present at the ceremony. The clergy, a surpliced choir and churchwardens stood to the west of the foundation-stone which was laid in the centre of the east wall, behind the site of the high altar. Miss Rolle, Lady Gertrude Rolle and other dignitaries stood to the east of the stone.

Upon the completion of the new church early in 1893, it was stated in the magazine *The Church in the West*, dated 29 April 1893, that the architect George Fellowes Prynne had 'designed a stately and beautiful building, worthy to rank among the finest modern churches in the country'. In the same article, the design of the church was described as being:

of Early English type, and the plan of the church is in the main cruciform, having a nave of five bays, ninety feet long by twenty-seven feet broad, north and south aisles, and transepts. The illustration of the building which we give today will enable our readers to form some opinion of its fine appearance. The tower and spire, which will reach a height of 140 feet are not yet erected. The interior aspect of the church is extremely dignified, the fine chancel – forty feet long – and the width of the nave, being especially so. An apsidal-ended chapel is placed on the south side of the chapel, and an organ chamber, gallery, and capacious vestries on the north side. The base of the tower forms a baptistry at the west end of the north aisle. Without entering into a detailed description of the church it may undoubtedly be described as costly and handsome. Externally, with its red tiled roofs, Devon limestone and marble facings, and dressings of Doulting stone, the appearance of the building, as it stands out of a background of green trees is extremely picturesque. It will look even better when the lofty tower and spire are erected. Internally the effect of the whole design is noble and dignified, the spacious nave and elevated chancel, with the richly vested altar, backed by the dossal hangings and side wings of embroidered cloth, contributing to the impressive appearance of this fine interior. This result is largely assisted by the costly and handsome fittings with which the new church has been supplied. The floor of the sanctuary is of polished marble, this beautiful stone being lavishly used throughout the building, which will seat 800.

In addition to the land and church donated by the Hon. Mark Rolle, other benefactors generously gave fittings for the inside of the church: Lady Rolle donated the high altar and the chancel screen of Beer stone and marble; Mrs Dart gave the pulpit; Mrs Baker gave the handsome oak litany desk; Misses Mary and Lucy Gardiner gave a processional cross and bier.

The Grand Opening and Consecration of St Peter's Church

Flags festooned Budleigh Salterton on Tuesday 25 April, the Feast of St Mark and the day of the grand opening and consecration of the new church. Conveyances of all types brought clergy and other folk from far and near to assist in the ceremony. Dr Bickersteth (the bishop of the diocese), the clergy and the choir put on their robes in the Rolle Chapel for the last time. They then moved in procession to the new church.

Opon their arrival at the west door of the new church Revd W.F. Green, the vicar, knocked three times. The architect, George Fellowes Prynne, opened the door and the procession proceeded up the nave. At the chancel entrance the people's churchwarden, Mr H.C. Perriam, presented the petition for the consecration of the new church which, upon being read by the registrar Mr Arthur Burch, was duly signed by the bishop. The customary service was followed with an offertory collection for the choir-stalls fund and for a new organ, to replace the old one from the chapel of ease. A total sum of £500 was subscribed.

The Hon. Mark Rolle was present throughout the service, as was the Lord-Lieutenant of the County, Lord Clinton. Visiting clergy had travelled from diverse places, such as Exmouth, Horrabridge, Lympstone, Exeter, Woodbury, Louth, Croydon, Otterton, Littleham, Bicton, Sherbourne, Colyton, Worcester, Kensington, Clysthydon, Ashburton and Offwell.

It is reported in *The Church in the West* that after the church services, there was a luncheon at the Public Rooms, which had been festooned with flags, banners and floral arrangements. The Hon. Mark Rolle presided over various toasts, speeches and responses. Mr H.G. Baker proposed a toast to the clergy of the parish. Revd Green responded to Mr Baker by saying that during his eight years in Budleigh Salterton, he had seen the following changes:

the communicants had increased from five per cent of the population to sixteen per cent, and their offertories had increased five-fold. They had in that period also raised, independent of the gift of Mr Rolle, £12,000 for church and Chapel-of-Ease purposes. They had restored one church, Mr Rolle had built another, and there was also a mission chapel at Knowle nearing completion. God's blessing on Church work in the district had been most marvellous during the last few years, and under it all difficulties and obstacles had disappeared. Laymen had been most ready with their help, and there appeared to be no end to their liberality. He had also had most hearty assistance and co-operation from his church workers.

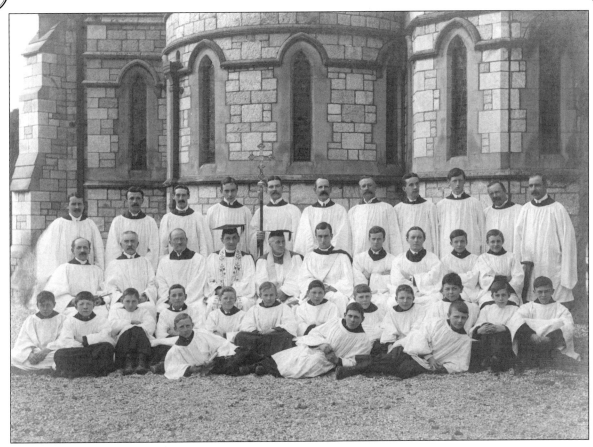

St Peter's Church Choir, 1930s. The photograph includes: *Mr Cowd* (back row, first from left), *George Annis* (back row, ninth from left) *and Len Curtis* (middle row, seventh from left). (St Peter's Church)

St Peter's Church Choir at Bury St Edmunds, 2000. Left to right, back row: *Rob Battershill, David Griffith, Martin Wooller, Roger Hennah, George Lisle, Chris Parrish, John Attwood, Philip Leat, Jim Birtwistle, Peter Cook, Robert Sellin, Peter Burness* (organist); front row: *Sylvia Pritchard (musical director), Janet Parrish, Fiona Hennah, Doris Godfrey, Sue Waddington, Jenny Battershill, Jane Briscoe, Jenny Steele, Mary Leat.*

(Philip Leat)

Revd Edmonds, vicar of St Peter's Church from 1918 to 1947, pictured here with church officials amongst whom are: George Frayne, Mr Harry, Mr Trayhurn (?), Mr Carter, Mr Mitchell, Mr Ilett, Captain Bone and George Beasley. (ST PETER'S CHURCH)

A public tea was attended by many parishioners in the afternoon and a further church service was held in the evening.

On May 24 1893, in connection with the consecration of St Peter's, the Hon. Mark Rolle organised a treat for the pupils of the Budleigh Salterton day-school and Sunday school. A total of 300 children with several teachers and friends attended a short service in St Peter's, after which they marched to the schools where an ample tea awaited them. The children then enjoyed various amusements until dusk when, after hearty cheers for Mr Rolle, they went home.

In the *Exeter Architectural Society Transactions* dated shortly after the completion of St Peter's, the new church is described as follows:

[St Peter's] amply repays one for any trouble taken in visiting it, and any one, if he pays that visit, will be able to draw one of those contrasts which the elder Pugin in his day was fond of doing. For you have the new church of St Peter and the old Chapel licensed for worship so near together, that anyone can see at a glance the marvellous difference between the 'it is' and the 'it was'.

A Reredos in Memory of Parishioners

A new reredos was erected in St Peter's Church in memory of those parishioners who 'had passed beyond the veil'. It was blessed by the Bishop of Crediton on 5 July 1931 before a large congregation. The work, costing £1,400, was funded through voluntary subscriptions without the need for direct appeal. Designed by Mr H.P. Burke of Westminster, the

St Peter's Church under restoration. The church suffered bomb damage on 17 April 1942, apparently from a single aircraft. (ST PETER'S CHURCH)

reredos had the adoration of the Saviour as its theme. The *Devon and Exeter Gazette*, dated July 1921, gives the following description:

The reredos, built of Ancaster stone, is some 18 feet high. The central figure of the Good Shepherd under a richly detailed canopy, with, at the foot, angels in the attitude of adoration, recalls our Lord's command to St Peter to 'feed my Sheep'. This is flanked by sculptured panels of the Annunciation and the Nativity. All the figure work is in high relief within a deeply recessed frame with cornice and cresting, and enriched with tracery and carving. Four central shields bear the emblems of the evangelists, and those on the right and left of these, the sacred monograms, the emblem of St Peter and the arms of the see of Exeter. The whole is an exceptionally beautiful example of the modelling and work of the veteran sculptor Mr Nathanial Hitch, of Vauxhall. The altar frame and riddel posts follow the English tradition. These are finely carved and decorated in gold and colour, and fitted with blue and silver silk tapestry panel and curtains. The four golden angels bearing lighted tapers which surmount the riddel posts are an exact reproduction by Messrs Barkentin and Krall of the medieval figures from Nurenburg [sic]. The stone reredos is flanked on both sides by foliated linenfold panelling in oak, which has been left in its natural colour.

In his address during the service, the bishop voiced his hope that despite the entrancing beauty of the reredos, parishioners would be able to relate to it on a much deeper level, than a purely aesthetic one. He also hoped it would represent dedication and sacrament, and have a mission of thankful joy.

The proposed tower and spire for St Peter's Church never rose above the height it was in 1893. It is said the tower and spire were to be completed at the expense of the parishioners. The area where bell-ringers would have stood to summon all to church is a baptisty at the time of writing.

Other Places of Worship

Prior to the building of the Catholic Church of St Peter, Prince of the Apostles, in 1927 at the expense of a Mr and Mrs Godfrey, the Catholics of Budleigh Salterton attended mass in the home of an old lady, situated where the health centre now stands. Mass was held in an upstairs room of the Public Hall when the house was demolished.

The Catholic Church of St Peter, a simple building, consists of a chancel, nave and vestry with open rafters to the roof. Later additions consisted of a porch, a small extension to house the organ and a side aisle. In the latter years of the twentieth century an external porch and a second larger vestry have improved church facilities.

The small Baptist chapel in Little Knowle was built in 1844 by public subscription. The Plymouth Brethren met in the Gospel Hall in Station Road.

References:

Beatrix F. Creswell MS, *Notes on Devon Churches, Deanery of Aylesbeare*, Westcountry Studies Library.

J. Davidson MS, *Churches in East Devon*, Westcountry Studies Library.

East Budleigh and Budleigh Salterton Parish Magazine (issues dating from the period 1874–1892).

Exeter Architectural Society Transactions, 3rd Series (1895), vol.1.

P. Hull, *The Catholic Church of St Peter, Prince of the Apostles* (local pamphlet).

The Church in the West (April 29, 1893).

The Universe (September 1935).

Trewman's *Exeter Flying Post*.

A.N. Walton, 'James Lackington and Methodism in Budleigh Salterton', *Proceedings of the Wesley Historical Society* (1932), vol.18.

White's *Directory of Devon, 1850* (A.M. Kelly, New York, 1968).

The interior of the Ebenezer Baptist Church. Churchgoers presented this photograph to Mr and Mrs Clode on the occasion of their golden wedding on 16 April 1948.

(BAPTIST CHURCH)

'Happiness' – a decorated arch at Knowle. This was probably for the wedding of Joan Peppis of Knowle House in the 1920s. The boy wearing an eye patch (fourth from right) *is Harry Bickley.* (STEVE RICHARDSON)

The Exeter and District Baptist Association spring meeting at Budleigh Salterton, 20 May 1954, with the Revd A. Lane as host to the visiting clergy.
(BAPTIST CHURCH)

'Health' – the other side of the wedding arch.
(KATH GOODING)

Schoolchildren with reverend gentlemen, 1930s.
(NICK LOMAN COLLECTION)

Chapter 9

◇

Education

Alongside the national schools, there was also an abundance of private schools and academies catering for day and boarding pupils in Budleigh Salterton during the nineteenth century. In his thesis, *A History of Budleigh Salterton Voluntary Schools, 1825–1954*, A.R. Lake states that Budleigh Salterton had, in social class terms, 'a top, a bottom and very little middle'. Thus the national schools catered for the offspring of the working-class poor, whilst the other schools were attended by the better-off sector of the population.

The national schools have survived in the form of St Peter's School, but many of the private schools and academies existed for only a short period of time. As a result, it has been possible to give a much fuller account of the national schools than their counter-

parts. It has, however, been possible to give a brief account of various educational establishments that lay within the town.

A Seminary for Young Ladies

In 1814 Miss Hine opened a seminary for a limited number of young ladies in Budleigh Salterton. Every attention was to be paid to their 'health, morals and improvement'. For a fee of 25 guineas per annum, each girl was instructed by the 'most approved masters' in subjects such as Grammar, Geography, the Use of the Globes, History, Dancing, French, Music and Drawing. In 1817, however, Miss Hine moved her school to Exmouth, as it was more convenient for the masters and stagecoach connections.

St Peter's School, 1920s. Left to right, back row: *Fred Solomon, Bill Harding, Richard Pitts, ? Davey, ?, Cyril Teed, Arthur Skinner;* middle row: *Harry Pyne, Ted Willoboughy, Albert Hill, Albert Watkins, ?;* front row: *Eddy Burch, ? Solomon, Jackie Bickley.*

(Kath Gooding)

A Brief Outline of Schooling in England in the Nineteenth and Twentieth Centuries

British schools, formed in 1808, were based on the monitorial system where the older children taught groups of younger ones under the supervision of paid staff.

National schools were formed in 1811 for the education of the poor according to the principles of the Established Church.

Dame schools were run by women as **elementary schools**, the fees being 3d. or 4d. per week. After the 1870 Education Act they began to disappear.

Forster's Education Act was passed in 1870. From this point onwards, England was to be divided into districts with boards being set up to manage each district. **Board schools** were the first schools to be run by local authorities. They could be secular and undenominational but an amendment called the Cowper-Temple Conscience Clause allowed schools to have religious instruction if they wished.

Legislation of 1876 made elementary education compulsory for all children. School attendance committees were set up where no school board existed.

The **Education Act of 1880** made school attendance compulsory up to the age of ten, at which time a child could leave on obtaining a certificate; if his record of attendance did not meet a required standard he had to stay at school for a longer period.

The **Education Act of 1889** set up the board of education. County Councils could levy a 1d. rate for technical education.

Legislation of 1891 made elementary education free. Legislation of 1893 and 1899 raised the school-leaving age to 11, then 12.

Balfour's Education Act of 1902 empowered local authorities to provide elementary and secondary education, superseding the old school boards.

As a result of the **Education Act of 1918** junior schools were established. They catered for 7–11 year olds whereas the earlier elementary schools had catered for 7–14 year olds.

Legislation in 1918 raised the school-leaving age to 14.

The **Education Act of 1944** abolished fees in state secondary schools. Elementary education was reorganised into infant and junior schools. Secondary education was graded into modern, grammar and technical schools and the school-leaving age was raised to 15.

The Budleigh Salterton Classical, Mathematical and Commercial Academy

The Budleigh Salterton Classical, Mathematical and Commercial Academy, conducted by Mr Chudleigh, was advertised in January 1849. The course of education offered to prospective students comprised the Classics, Mathematics, English Grammar, Writing, Arithmetic, Algebra, Merchants' Accounts, Geography, History, Mapping and the Use of the Globe, Astronomy and Elocution.

In the advertisement it was stated that the encouraging support Mr Chudleigh had received during the previous five years was 'sufficient proof of his undeviating endeavours to promote the welfare of the pupils entrusted in his care'. In the words of the advert, Budleigh Salterton is described as 'healthily situated, much admired and frequented as a watering-place', thus reminding the reader that the site of the school was both fashionable and beneficial to pupils' health.

The Belgrave College

The Belgrave College, of which a Mr Clarke was principal in 1866, prepared 'the sons of gentleman' for public schools, universities and the Oxford and Cambridge examinations. The college and grounds commanded extensive views of the country and sea and were within five minutes of the latter.

The Band of Hope

During the latter half of the nineteenth century, the Band of Hope held 'Industrial Classes' for girls on Wednesdays, whilst the boys' classes were on Wednesdays and Thursdays. Funds were raised through subscription and sales. A winter season opened with a choral service in St Peter's Church that was followed by a presentation of prizes won by pupils during the previous year. These were for proficiency 'in the several departments of industrial art', as well as regular attendance and good conduct.

Cliff Terrace Day and Boarding School

Arthur Roberts advertised in the *East Budleigh and Budleigh Salterton Parish Magazine* during 1889 that he had much experience in teaching and was receiving 6–14-year-old pupils for instruction in Arithmetic, Algebra, Latin, Greek, French and the usual English subjects. Special arrangements could be made for

German and Drawing. Mrs Roberts, who likewise had teaching experience, received a few young girls for tuition in English, French and Arithmetic.

The school was at Cliff Terrace where terms for day pupils under ten years of age was 2–3 guineas, and over ten years of age, 4 guineas. The fees for day boarders amounted to 7–8 guineas, whilst boarding fees were 12–15 guineas per term.

Fisher's School (Copplestone House Preparatory School for Girls)

During the 1920s Miss Tucker and Miss Lumby ran a Preparatory School for Girls at Copplestone House. It was later taken over by Miss Brackenbury and existed until 1943. The school was transferred to 'Braywick' in Bedlands Lane where Mr E. Fisher had run a Preparatory School for Boys until 1928.

From a report dated Monday 25 July 1932 within the pages of *The Times*, we find that the Bishop of Malmesbury had attended the school's prize-giving day on the previous Thursday. During his address to the school following the prize-giving, the bishop emphasized the importance of encouraging individuality in children. The home, he stated, was the chief factor in our national life and he urged the necessity of training girls early in domestic subjects in order that they should be competent home-makers.

Lansdowne Road Moorcroft Residential School

The catalogue of the Public Records Office at Kew records the existence of a residential school for evacuees with mental disabilities in Budleigh Salterton. The rather brutally named 'Lansdowne Road Moorcroft Residential School for Evacuated Mentally Defective Children' was in existence from 1941–44.

The National Schools

The nineteenth century saw great activity with regard to establishing an education system in England. In 1808 Joseph Lancaster, a Quaker, formed the Royal Lancastrian Society to promote his educational ideas. In 1810, the name of the society was changed to the British and Foreign School Society. Children were taught by means of the monitorial system i.e. the older pupils taught the younger ones under the supervision of paid staff. Other types of schools also adopted this system. In 1811 the National Society for the Education of the Poor in the Principles of the Established Church was

Class of 1921, St Peter's School. Left to right, back row: *Flo Hillman, Nellie Snell, Edith Marker, Sissy Mears, ?, Emmy Walley, May Chapman, Ruth Pearcey;* middle row: *Cynthia Marks, ?, ?, ?, Edith Watkins, ?, Gladys Sedgemore, Vera Knowles, Dorothy Haslem, Violet Hitt, Mary Pratt, Madge Christopher, ?;* front row: *? Marker, ?, Lilly Bastin, Florrie Harris, Amy Trick, Peggy Southcott, Elsie Sanders, Joan Mann, Edith Brooks, Ena Cooper, Kathleen Burch.* (KATH GOODING)

Girls of Miss Manning's school celebrate the end of the Second World War on The Green. The photograph includes: *Marian Veale, Nellie Beer, the Elliot twins, Janet Trump, Mary Clarke, Ann Sellick, Shirley Delaney, Joan Searle.* (NICK LOMAN COLLECTION)

A class of 1902, Queen Street Schools. Mr Griffin (far left, back row) was the headmaster.
(KATH GOODING)

formed and, with the patronage of Lord Rolle, the formation of a national school came about in Budleigh Salterton in 1825. No evidence appears as to where this school was situated.

The Monitorial System

Pupil monitors were used during the early years of the Budleigh Salterton schools. A small remuneration was paid to them for their efforts, for example in the year 1887 a payment of £4.10s. was paid to them out of the school's income. One Devon head teacher, however, thought little of the monitorial system, saying of his pupils 'few make good monitors, they do but little and often harm'.

Teaching Staff

One of the earliest schoolmasters at Budleigh Salterton was a Mr Churchill. He was followed by Charles Westcomb, a son of a bricklayer born in Paris Street in Exeter in 1821. Westcomb had been educated at St Sidwell's School, where he was described as 'being a bright boy, particularly with figures'. At the age of 19 he was appointed headmaster at Budleigh Salterton, with a salary of £30 per year. A house was provided for his accommodation in addition to the salary. Westcomb stayed at Budleigh Salterton for 15 years before returning to Exeter in 1855.

The National Schools, Queen Street

Under Westcomb, the schools moved into the Queen Street premises. White's *Directory* of 1850 informs us that these premises, 'a neat National School', had been built by the late Lord Rolle in 1842. The school was later divided into two, separating boys from girls, with Theophilida Blatchford as schoolmistress alongside Westcomb. By 1856 Sidney Smith and Caroline Williams had taken over. In 1870 James Atwell and Henrietta Atwell were in situ.

In 1846/7, 62 boys were taught in a classroom which was 37ft long, 17ft wide and 8ft high; 43 girls were taught in a separate classroom of similar proportions. The master's accommodation consisted of a parlour, kitchen, scullery and two bedrooms. The schools were supported by an income of £46 from private subscriptions, £23 from local donations and £12 in children's pence (a sum of money paid by the children's parents). Expenditure amounted to £34 for the schoolmaster, £28 to the schoolmistress, £1 for fuel and light and £15 rent for the school building.

Forster's Education Act of 1870

Forster's Education Act was the topic discussed at a meeting at the Rolle Arms on 26 November 1870.

After various discussions between Mr Lipscombe (the Rolle Estate steward), and the ratepayers attending the meeting, it was decided to adjourn until 10 December. At a second meeting Mr Lipscombe informed the ratepayers that Mr Rolle would hand the school over to the inhabitants of Budleigh Salterton on the following terms:

That the school be conducted on the voluntary system, so as to secure a sound religious instruction, with the protection of the Conscience Clause.
That the school be managed by a Committee consisting of the Vicar, Curate, Churchwarden, himself (or his representative), and three others, to be elected by the subscribers, who would have votes according to the amount of their subscriptions.
That the school be entirely at the disposal of the clergymen of Budleigh Salterton on Sundays.
That the foregoing stipulations be cancelled in the event of the election of a School Board.

There was an almost unanimous show of hands in favour of Mr Rolle's offer, after which Mr Lipscombe stated that Mr Rolle and Lady Rolle would subscribe £15.15s. to the Budleigh Salterton schools.

School Inspections

The diocesan inspection of the Budleigh Salterton schools, held on 27 May 1880, reported that the religious knowledge of the schools was good. Lord Rolle had therefore secured his wish that there was to be 'a sound religious instruction' at the schools.

Inspectors reported in January 1887 that 67 boys and 64 girls had been examined. As many as 98 per cent of boys and 100 per cent of girls passed in reading; singing was fair; discipline and order was rated as good. The girls' needlework was also good, the sale of which had raised the sum of £4.15s.6d. The school was awarded government grants amounting to £182.3s.6d., including the highest possible grants for English and Geography.

At the Infants' School, elementary subjects were deemed to be well taught. There were lessons on Form, Colour and Objects. Singing was rated as good, as was needlework; discipline and order were rated as satisfactory. The sum of £6.17s.2d. was paid out in bonuses for good attendance.

In the diocesan inspector's report of 1889, the following was stated of the boys' school:

This is one of the best Schools I have ever examined. The repetition was said with perfect accuracy and excellent expression and the answering was bright and intelligent.

St Peter's School, 1955. Left to right, back row: *Mary Davie, Faith Evans, Mary Bapstone ?, ? Spargo, ? Pyne, ?, ?;* third row: *?, ?, Joey Gather, Joan Pearman, ?, Susan Bond, ?, Steve Brooks, ?;* second row: *? Hinman, Anthony Watkins, Adrian Spiller, Rodney Paver, Chris Miller, ? Smith, ? Parker, Cyril Rooke, Tom Whitfield;* front row: *Nick and Bob Loman, ? Hinman, Phillip Clemence, ?, David Williams, Rodney Wilkinson.*

(NICK LOMAN COLLECTION)

St Peter's School netball team, 1960/61. Left to right, back row: *Penny Edds, Doreen Oakes, Mrs Harrison, Jenny Brown, Kay Clarke;* front row: *Rosemary Smith, Linda Marker, Linda Spiller.*

(NICK LOMAN COLLECTION)

The physical state of the Budleigh Salterton schools was, however, called into question by the school inspectors in 1892:

Ventilation might be improved... The desks are very old, flat, and too low, especially for the elder boys. The access to the offices [toilets] entirely throughout the School is very unsuitable. A porch for caps, etc, is needed.

The cost of replacing the desks was £27. It was hoped the school managers could induce subscribers 'to be very generous', in order to meet the needs of the school inspectors 'for the comfort of the children' and 'aiding the teachers in their arduous work'. By 1892 it was reported that 'great improvement' had been effected on the premises which were by then 'quite satisfactory'.

Owing to a 'long prevailing sickness' in 1894 the schools were closed under 'medical order'. The Education Department waived the annual inspection due in January 1895 so government grants were made as in the previous year.

The Early-Twentieth Century

In 1906 the Queen Street schools could cater for 250 children; an average of 70 boys, 65 girls and 70 infants attended. The schools were endowed with £32 from Drake's charity. Thomas Henry Griffin was the master (1880–1912); Miss Elizabeth Burgess was mistress, with Miss Eva Sargent as the infants' mistress. Six managers controlled the schools. At this time the school at Knowle catered for 40 infants, and the average attendance was only 14 pupils. Miss Alice Spurway was the mistress and the school was controlled by six managers.

By this time, the physical state of the Budleigh Salterton schools was once again cause for concern. The school inspectors regularly complained about the lack of space, poor playground facilities and the use of the playground by a neighbouring washerwoman as a 'drying area' for her customers' clothes. Parents were worried about the sanitation and kept their children away from the schools in hot weather because of the 'drains and the smell they emitted'. In 1911 the Queen Street schools were condemned. During these times lice became a common complaint in Devon schools, with 40 per cent of pupils being affected yet, for some reason, only 20 per cent of children were allowed treatment by parents.

A New Site

Tom Griffin, the well-liked and long-serving headmaster, who had been at the schools during the troublesome times died in 1912 after a short illness. Frank Mullis, his successor, took the schools to a new site in 1913, thanks to land donated by Lord Rolle. A new building costing nearly £30,000 was erected with money from local subscriptions, bazaars held at Exeter, as well as donations from Drake's and Hine's charities, the National Society and the Diocesan Council.

The new site, criticised by the local people as being too remote from the town, was worth £500. Lord Clinton officially opened the new schools on 17 April 1913, stressing that he felt that 'not too much money should be spent on buildings as it was better spent on real education work'.

The school consisted of three departments each with their own entrances, cloakrooms, stores and teachers' rooms. The school could accommodate 298 pupils (80 boys, 80 girls and 138 infants). There were seven classrooms, two of which could be made into one large room with seating for 165 pupils. The spacious playgrounds (the girls' had a maypole) had large 'play sheds' open to the sunshine where the children sometimes ate their dinner of 'bread, jam and a cup of water'. Latrine units were independent and of the flushing type. Mr J.W. Palmer of Budleigh Salterton carried out the building works.

The old Queen Street school buildings became known as the Parish Rooms and were used for Domestic Science lessons, dances, elections and the like. They were eventually replaced by two cottages and a garage.

Problems Between the Schools

Although the boys' and girls' schools worked together, there was occasionally friction between them. One particular irritation noted in the infants' logbook on 19 November 1914 was that 'The value of the carefully prepared scripture lesson this morning was rendered practically nil by the noise in the boys' playground'. Arguments continued, culminating with a dramatic incident, entered in the infants' logbook on 21 July 1915:

The Head Mistress was this afternoon assaulted by the Headmaster of the Boys School, who pushed her violently and turned a water tap upon her, drenching her to the skin!

A letter of apology came from the headmaster.

Sport

In the 1920s the boys' school was very successful in the local schools' football league. The team won the Morrison Bell Cup, an achievement which was considered so remarkable that the town band leading a grand parade welcomed the victorious team home.

Discipline
In 1921 the school inspectors complained 'that some girls are only punished verbally'. The mistress therefore caned several girls 'as suggested by the Inspectors'. As a consequence of this the girls stayed away from school with the full support of their parents, whereupon the mistress promptly resigned.

Restructuring of the Schools
The year 1936 was an eventful one for the Budleigh Salterton schools. The pupils were divided between a Junior Mixed and Infants' Department and a Senior Department. The Junior Department, with 131 pupils on the roll, had Miss Bond as head. She was supported by four teachers, three certificated and one uncertificated. The Senior Department had 103 pupils with Mr Taylor as head. He was supported by three full-time certificated teachers, with part-time Woodwork and Domestic Science teachers. At this time East Budleigh and Otterton transferred their senior pupils to Budleigh Salterton.

In the same year, the canteen was completed, upon which 54 children sat down to school dinners for the first time on 14 September 1936. Indoor toilets were installed and a telephone was also provided.

The Second World War
With war looming, an entry in the logbook dated 27 September 1938 reads 'The work was interfered with today. The Head Teacher was fitting children with gas masks'. Throughout the war years the school premises were used according to a shift system, whereby the locals could use the school from 9a.m. to 1p.m. and the visitors (evacuees) from 1.30p.m. to 5.30p.m. With children numbering over 600, the guide hut, drill hall, Public Hall, church institute and the Baptist schoolroom were also used. The evacuee children were from Bristol, Fulham and Croydon.

Special efforts were made at the school in connection with the war effort: 'Wings for Victory' week raised £227 on 11 June 1943; 'Salute the Soldier' week raised £228 on 22 May 1944.

St Peter's School
On 9 April 1954 Budleigh Salterton schools ceased to cater for all ages; the seniors were transferred to Exmouth secondary schools. The school at Budleigh Salterton reopened as St Peter's School, a voluntary primary school, with 259 pupils on the roll.

References
East Budleigh and Budleigh Salterton Parish Magazine (various issues).

Kelly's *Directory*, 1897.

A.R. Lake, *A History of Budleigh Salterton Voluntary Schools, 1825–1954* (Exeter, 1974, Thesis (Dip. Ed.), Exeter University, School of Education.

J. Richardson, *The Local Historian's Encyclopedia* (New Barnet, Historical Publications, 1986.)

Trewman's *Exeter Flying Post* (editions from November and December 1870).

White's *Directory of Devon*, 1850.

St Peter's School football team, 1928/29.

(Steve Richardson)

St Peter's School netball team, winners of the Devon and Cornwall Constabulary 1990 School Sports Competition. The back row includes: Mrs Pauline Michael (teacher and coach) and Mr George Lisle (headmaster). Left to right, middle row: Hazel Brown, Hannah Farley, Francesca Hitt, Katrina May, Emily Rorke, Jennifer Hardman; front row: Denise Payne, Emma Davey, Lucy Loman. (NICK LOMAN COLLECTION)

St Peter's School football team 1926/27. Left to right, back row: Mr Cornish, Edward Pearcey, Michael ?, ? Annis, Jim Harris, Bill Clark, Mr Williams; middle row: Albert Watkins, Sid Matthews, Fred Trick, George Palmer, Leslie Burch; sitting on the floor: Bert Watts. (KATH GOODING)

St Peter's School football team 1989/90. Left to right, back row: *Graham May, John Dack, Tim Asby, David Hindel, Ian Hooper;* front row: *Andrew Dack, Matthew Sanders, Daniel Crookel, Matthew Chown, Lloyd Loman.*
(NICK LOMAN COLLECTION)

Girls of St Peter's School, 1924. Left to right, back row: *Jessie Lane, Joan Baker, Iris Waller, Ann Marker, Lillian Pearcey, Phyllis Skinner, Peggy Milne;* front row: *Sylvia Watkins, Ethel Morris, Phyllis Davie, Joyce Dowell;* sitting on grass: *Ivy Waller.*
(KATH GOODING)

Chapter 10

A Miscellany of Topics

Poetic Salterton

An anonymous article appearing in the *Express and Echo* dated July 1937 tells us that:

The charming characteristics of Budleigh Salterton can be easily accepted as sources of inspiration for poetic fancies that do not hide themselves in booklets for private circulation, but are exhibited for public enjoyment, and, possibly, adroit admonition.

Apparently, whilst on an unplanned visit to Budleigh Salterton, a correspondent (possibly the author of the above article) fortuitously stumbled upon two rather humorous pieces of poetry. One of the poems was found on the wall enclosing the grounds of the former vicarage, on the road to Exmouth. Engraved on a tablet of stone were the following words:

Give this house, oh traveller pray,
A blessing as you pass this way;
And if you've time, I beg your pardon,
While you're at it, bless the garden.

From the age of the material and lettering it was thought that the poetry was probably not the work of a vicar, but could instead be attributed to a lay resident from a former period.

Carnival fancy dress, 1956, with Alan Deller, Miss Ivings? and Kay Clarke.   (NICK LOMAN COLLECTION)

Budleigh Salterton Games Club, 1930s. Left to right, back row: *Mr Webber, Mr Hammond, Mr Marks?, ?, ?, ?, Mr Clemens, Mr Freeman, Mr Anderson?, Sam Ashword, ?;* front row: *?, ?, Harry Carter, ?, Revd Edmonds, Mr McGowan, Mr Pike, ?, Jimmy Green.* (KATH GOODING)

Fun at Fairlynch, 1987. Left to right, back row: *Donna Crook?, Haley Lemon, Pippa Brown;* front row: *Lucy Saunders, ?, Emily Saunders.* (JULIA MEREDITH)

Girl Guides, Queen Street, c.1919. The photograph includes: Dorothy Davie, Amy Gooding, Alice Marker, Dorothy Sanders, Connie Pratt, Josephine Blackburn, Dorothy Haslem, Winnie Bastin, Nellie Pearcey, Elsie Sanders, Lilly White, Hilda French, Kath Gooding, Dorothy Bucknell, Mrs Foster, Lady Clinton, Mrs Bond, Miss Addington, Gerty Cooper, Jessie Southcott, Betty Curtis, Amy Pratt, Daisy Watkins, Emmy Walley, Edith Ilett, Peggy Southcott, Olive Sedgemore. (KATH GOODING)

Ladies' tug of war, Knowle, 1935. The ladies on the rope are, left to right: *Kath Gooding, Edie Watts, ?, ?, Dorry Watts, Mrs Sage, Mrs Pinney, Lilly Heard.* (KATH GOODING)

Church Parade, Station Road, 1954. Taking part are the Life Boys, Scouts, Cubs, Girl Guides and Brownies.
The photograph also includes: *Nick Loman, Mr and Mrs Hawkes, Rodney Wilkinson, Len Clarke, Cyril Rooke, Francis Bedford, Mrs Partridge and Carol Deller.* (NICK LOMAN COLLECTION)

Boys' Brigade, 1957. The photograph includes: Chris Loman, Colin Yates, Colin Martin, Nick Loman, Steve Brooks, ? Davie, Frank Selly, Peter Tanton, Bob Loman, Dave Veale, Mr Edds and Mr Bumpstead.
(NICK LOMAN COLLECTION)

The second poem, found on the gate of a house on the road towards East Budleigh, recited:

Be ye man or be ye woman,
Be ye early or be ye late,
Be ye comin' or be ye goin'
Be ye sure and shut this gate.

Doubtless these humorous words were more effective in persuading visitors to comply with the resident's request than the usual 'Please shut the gate'.

A Riddle

The following riddle entitled 'Enigma to be Answered' was also inspired by Budleigh Salterton:

My whole is a stream sweet as any could wish,
And yet I'm a creature that preys upon fish;
My last, first, and fourth, in the fish you will find,
And yet 'tis a creature as fleet as the wind,
My third, first, and last, the Dartmoor hills crown
My third, first, last and fourth, make you mend up your own,
My second and first sound like twice one, although
There is one letter short of course you should know,
My first, fourth, and fifth, lies above mostly found,
My first, fifth and fourth lies beneath the hard ground,
My first you will use if you speak when in pain,
My third you will take after dinner again,
My third, first, and my fourth, you each one have got,
My last, first, and third, I would hope you know not,
Four letters yet five, my whole word do compose,
And yet I spell ten words or more I suppose,
But if you can't guess me ashamed I would be,
For often at Salterton you have seen me.

This riddle, penned by R.C.P., still rings true over 100 years after it first appeared in the *East Budleigh and Budleigh Salterton Parish Magazine* of 1888. (The answer to this riddle can be found on p.160.)

A Big Catch

The Times dated 12 September 1930 reported that:

A blue shark was caught on rod and line at Budleigh Salterton. Mr Hugh Chaddock, with Mr George Pearcy, a local fisherman, were half a mile out at sea fishing for conger eel when the shark was seen 'playing about'. Half a mackerel was placed on the line, and it was quickly swallowed by the shark. It took three-parts of an hour to play the shark out, when it was brought close to shore and gaffed by other local fishermen. It

A view of the Budleigh Salterton cricket ground, 1930s.
(NICK LOMAN COLLECTION)

The Budleigh Salterton cricket ground whilst under water, Boxing Day, 1956. (NICK LOMAN COLLECTION)

weighed 2½cwt., was 7 feet 1 inch in length, and had a 2 feet 6 inch tail.

The Public Rooms

From Kelly's *Directory of Devon* for 1897 we find that a building called the Public Rooms, situated on the 'West Road' near the Masonic Hall, was opened in February 1862, with a capital of £750 being raised in £5 shares. There were commodious committee rooms with a residence for a caretaker. The architectural style was Italian, with cement mouldings and façades. The main room was capable of holding 500 people. A public dinner celebrated the event. The building's demise came about when it suffered bomb damage during the Second World War.

Husbands Galore

'Volo Non Valeo', author of *We Donkeys In Devon* published in 1886, imparts that 'a sketch of Budleigh Salterton would be very imperfect' without reference to a 'remarkable man and his more remarkable wife'.

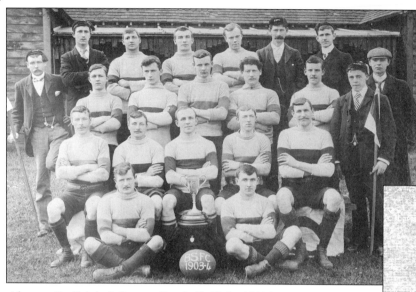

Above: *Budleigh Salterton Football Club, 1903/4, winners of the 'Herbert' Cup and joint holders of the Devon County Junior 'Medal' Championship.* Left to right, back row: *A. Teed, G. Annis, J.A. Williams, L.A. Balkwill, G. Burroughs, R. Annis, R. Kingdom;* third row: *W. Bickley, W.J. Mears, J. Palmer, W. Pearcey, W.R. Bennett, C.H. Trickey;* second row: *E. Knight, J. Pearcey, E. Bennett (captain), W.J. Pratt, F. Teed, C.J. Horrill;* front row: *A.G. Baker, B. Stamp.* (TOM OAKES)

Right: *The official fixtures list of the Budleigh Salterton Football Club, 1933/34.* (TOM OAKES)

Budleigh Salterton

FOOTBALL

CLUB

❖❖

OFFICIAL FIXTURES, 1933-34

❖❖

President:
MAJOR H. NUTHALL.

Vice-Presidents:

Sir Fredk. Fowke	Mr. F. G. Hill
Col. S. Aplin. C.S.I.	„ M. Richardson
Lt.-Col. Allin	„ J. Keslake
Major W. Meldon	„ G. E. Arundel
Capt. C. B. Bone	„ H. W. Adie
Capt. J. W. Palmer	„ S. R. Baker
Air Commander Gossage	„ H. P. Perriam
Dr. H. Semple	„ K. Voss
Dr. T. Evans	„ McIntosh
Dr. Vincent Smith	„ H. Carter
Mr. H. C. Bennett	„ Pearse
Mr. Hamilton Hudson	

Budleigh Salterton Football Club 1959/60. Left to right, back row: *Charlie Bray, Mr Thorpe, George Gooch, Freddie Vanstone, Bill Knowles, John Mills, Fred Knowles, Nora Thomas, Mrs Thorpe, Kath Gooding, Billy Veale;* front row: *Frank Hill, Gerald Rooke, Tom Power, Brian Vinnicombe, Stan Corfield (with cup), Peter Hillman, Colin Pannel, Terry Paver, Les Pratt.* (KATH GOODING)

Budleigh Salterton Football Club presentation, Boxing Day, 1962. Left to right, back row: *Jim Everest, Alfie Pyle;* front row: *Kath Gooding, Tom Deller* (with clock), *Mr Hamer.* (KATH GOODING)

Mr Lackington, benefactor of The Temple, and his wife are the couple in question.

A native of Taunton, Mr Lackington went to London as a young man where he followed the trade of cobbler. In addition to his manual skills, Lackington must have possessed an intuitive commercial mind. He made £5 from selling penny books alongside his cobbling, and then set himself up as a bookseller. With a turnover of 100,000 books yearly, he managed to secure himself a large fortune.

He returned to Taunton in 1806 where he became the object of a young lady's affections, despite the fact that she was already engaged to a man her own age. Her fiancé insisted that their wedding should go ahead, however, during the ceremony she declined his hand when the crucial question was asked and walked out of the church. She then married Mr Lackington, and the newly-weds moved to Budleigh Salterton. Mr Lackington died at the age of 70 on 22 November 1815 and was buried at East Budleigh.

Mrs Lackington found solace by marrying a Mr Symes at East Budleigh in 1817. He died and was buried at East Budleigh. She married again in 1822. Her third husband, named Gellard, along with her two previous spouses, was also buried at East Budleigh. In 1834 she married a Mr Manley, and upon his death he too was buried at East Budleigh. So here we have a woman who not only married three times in the same church, but laid to rest four of her husbands in the surrounding graveyard.

She left Budleigh Salterton after the death of Mr Manley and moved to Exeter where at the age of 70 she became attached to a young shopman. On this occasion, however, she did not wed her man – she thought him too young and gave him £50 'in lieu of her hand'.

A Cornishman by the name of Huddy became

aware of her allure and her income of £500 per year. He travelled to Exeter and married her, whereupon they went to live in Cornwall. This particular venture was not to her liking; she left him and went back to Exeter. A congenial arrangement was made whereby her husband was given £50 a year during her remaining lifespan.

This woman had been engaged to be married seven times, had come to the altar six times and entered the holy estate of matrimony five times. According to 'Volo Non Valeo', she was, 'without doubt, the most remarkable person who ever lived in Budleigh Salterton'. 'Volo Non Valeo' was Miss Maria Gibbons, who lived in Victoria Place and drove about in a donkey carriage.

A Smoking Concert

'A most successful Smoking Concert – the first, we believe ever given in Budleigh Salterton and the first we hope of a series...' This was the opening line of a report about a 'Smoking Concert' held at the Church House, Budleigh Salterton, on 23 February 1889.

Attended by around 35 male members of St Peter's Church, who apparently 'evinced their enjoyment by joining most heartily in the choruses and songs'. The repertoire included two readings by Mr Friend and the following songs: 'Sailing' performed by Mr Squire; 'Four Jolly Smiths', Mr Sanders; 'The Bay of Biscay', Mr Lethbridge; 'Ring the Bell Watchman', Mr Newberry; 'Father O'Flynn', Mr Squire; 'Hearts of Oak', Mr Sargent; 'A Little Farm Well Till'd', Mr Griffin, Mr Newberry and Mr Squire; 'John Peel', Mr Webber; 'Now We've Got a Baby', Mr Newberry; 'Tenting On the Old Camp Ground', Mr Sanders and quartette; 'Two in the Morning', Mr Squire.

Coffee and tobacco were enjoyed by the participants throughout the evening. The Revd Price gave a speech towards the end and, after passing some humorous remarks on smoking and smokers, said that he had often wanted to get the men together in such a fashion. Although he had heard of smoking concerts, he had not known exactly what they involved. With the mystery unravelled, Revd Price trusted that repeat performances would be possible.

Mr Squire, the organiser of the event, suggested that some form of institution was lacking in Budleigh Salterton where they could all meet as 'good neighbours and good churchmen'. In his opinion, what was needed was the following:

a Church Institute, which should embrace Reading, Smoking, Bagatelle, and Class Rooms, a Cricket and Football Club, and above all a Musical Society – a home in fact of mutual recreation and improvement where they could meet regularly throughout the winter months for such entertainments as they had had to-night, and also for entertainments in which their wives and sweethearts could join in.

The evening culminated in the singing of 'God save the Queen'.

Property for Auction

The Rolle Arms was the venue for an auction on Monday 19 April 1830. The lot in question was a 'most desirable family residence', recently built and very substantial, situated near the chapel. The house was described as being 'admirably arranged under the immediate eye of the late owner', a Colonel John Tomkyns.

Undoubtedly one of the better detached houses in Budleigh Salterton at the time, the ground floor comprised an entrance hall, vestibule and staircase, dining-room (approx. 16ft sq.) with a sideboard recess and a drawing-room (16ft by 18ft). There was also a library (approx. 15ft by 13ft), butler's pantry, kitchen, servants' hall, back staircase and offices, not to mention a wine and beer cellar.

On the first floor were four bedrooms and dressing-rooms, a servant's room and water closet. Rooms on the ground floor were 11ft high whilst those on the first floor were 9ft high.

The house had a broad veranda on three sides, a private entrance and also a carriage entrance, spacious court-yard, coach-house and two-stalled stable and gardens. There was also a large garden on the opposite side of the road.

The situation of the house was indeed unrivalled; the expansive sea views included Tor Bay, Berry Head, Portland etc., but the house itself was sheltered

Above: *Budleigh Salterton boys on the beach, 1954.* Left to right: *Ginger Bridgewood, Courtney Richards, Stefan Brooks, Robert Chard, Nick Loman, Alan Deller, Bob Loman, Peter Deller, Paul Hind.*

(Nick Loman Collection)

enough to make it 'not only a summer, but a most comfortable winter residence for an invalid'. The proximity of the bathing machines, along with the desirability of the neighbourhood rendered it both 'convenient and generally admired'.

The premises were held under lease from Lord Rolle for the usual Devonshire term of three lives (or 99 years), with the right to add a fourth. This was often the case with properties in Devon. Tenants paid a 'fine' on acquiring the property, followed by an annual rent. A 'heriot' was then paid on the death of each life. The paying of heriots stemmed from Saxon times, when heirs were obliged to return the military apparel of a deceased tenant to the lord, on the assumption that it had been granted to the deceased by the lord in the first place. The apparel could include a horse, harness and weapons, according to the status of the tenant. This burden applied to both freeman and villeins, but by later periods tended to be pertinent to copyhold tenures only. The custom was superseded at about the time of the Norman Conquest by the gift of a best beast; this later became a money payment instead. The heriot was in effect a means of charging the heir to 'enter' the land and was not abolished until 1922.

Tragedies and Near Tragedies

During July 1770, two brothers along with their cousin went bathing at Budleigh Salterton whereupon an observant child noticed that they were in distress. The child immediately called for assistance, and the father of the two brothers, Mr Wensley, rushed to their rescue. Tragically, both brothers and their cousin drowned.

Budleigh Salterton resident, Mr Fouracres, was much more fortunate. It was reported in Trewman's *Exeter Flying Post* that whilst returning from a journey on horseback in May 1824, he decided 'most imprudently to cross the passage from The Warren to Exmouth when the tide was flowing with a strong ebb' and was unseated from his horse whilst doing so. Luckily for him two boats were nearby, otherwise he would certainly have drowned. Mr Staple and Mr Tilbury, along with two watermen, came to his rescue 'as he was on the point of sinking to rise no more'.

Four years later to the month, Trewman's *Exeter Flying Post* reported how the village of Budleigh Salterton had been 'thrown into a state of agitation in consequence of a report that a lady had attempted to destroy herself by poison'. It was said that 'from feelings of a too delicate a nature to touch upon' she procured 4oz of laudanum from the chemist and

Budleigh Salterton Swimming Club at the bottom of Steamer Steps, 1913. The photograph includes: *Mr Creedy* (with the ball) *and George Annis* (back row, first on the left). (NICK LOMAN COLLECTION)

The Budleigh Salterton Cricket Club youth team, 1958. Left to right, back row: *Reg Bourne, Phil Clements, Adrian Spiller, ?, Bob Loman, Chris Miller, ?;* middle row: *Jonathon Lee, Nick Loman, ?, ?, ?;* front row: *Nick Carter, Jim Callendar.* (NICK LOMAN COLLECTION)

during the early part of the evening 'rashly took the whole'. Surgeons Adams and Greatwood upon being called, attended to her throughout the night. By the following morning the 'unhappy woman' was pronounced to be out of danger.

One Sunday morning in May 1846 John Webber, a pilot, with two others, were engaged in catching mackerel at Budleigh Salterton when 'a sea' struck their boat and capsized her. Webber, although a very good swimmer and 'a daring fellow', drowned, possibly because the boat had hit his back. The other two men were saved. The deceased's father was the first to hear of the death of his son upon the news of the drowning reaching the town.

Another sad accident, which occurred just prior to the Christmas of 1896, cast gloom over festive rejoicings. It was reported in the *East Budleigh and Budleigh Salterton Parish Magazine* that three little boys lost their lives at Budleigh Salterton on 19 December. The brothers Arthur and Cecil Hitt, eight and six years of age respectively, were playing in a 'cubby-hole' under the West Cliff, with eight-year-old Percy Freeman, when all three were buried by a sudden landslide. It was hoped that they died instantly, and 'were spared all bodily pain and fear as they passed from their life on earth to their new and happy life in Paradise'. A large number of friends attended the funeral on Christmas Eve to pay their respects to the three boys who 'lay side by side in one grave, awaiting a joyful Resurrection'.

Death by Poison?

William Jones, who had been blind for seven or eight years, died during July 1863 at the age of 33. After his death, various rumours circulated that the former musician in the 16th Lancers had actually been poisoned by his wife. As a consequence of these rumours the coroner ordered a post mortem examination and an inquest which was held at the Rolle Arms.

Elizabeth Jones, the wife of the deceased, stated that they had been married for three years. On the morning of his death, her husband had not risen at the usual hour, complaining of a violent headache. He became sick and vomited, but because he had suffered similar attacks in the past she did not send for his doctor. When her husband's condition worsened, she called Dr Murphy. That evening her husband called her to his side, and said, 'I am dying, I am dying; may the Lord take my life'. Shortly afterwards he expired.

During the previous evening he had drunk a glass of beer and ate a little bread and cheese. She was not aware of having given him anything of a poisonous nature. He had, however, often complained that she gave him different meals to those she herself ate, but she attributed this to his blindness as they had always eaten the same meals. Mrs Jones confirmed that her husband had suffered fits on many previous occasions.

Dr Murphy said he had attended the deceased for five months and, after having been called by his wife, had found him dying from a suspected apoplectic fit. This diagnosis was later confirmed by the results of a post-mortem examination, which also established that the blindness of the deceased had been occasioned by a similar fit. As a result of this evidence, the jury found Elizabeth Jones not guilty of murder.

Budleigh Salterton Football Club, 1928/29. Left to right, back row: *Ted Hampstead, Walter Marker, ?, Bob Pratt, Fred Shepherd, Basil Hexter, Sid Moore, Charlie Mears, Stanley Keslake, ?, ?, Tom Hooker, George Annis, ?, George Frain;* front row: *?, Fred Veale, Monty Keslake, ? Pearcey, Bill Paver.* (KATH GOODING)

A Plea for Charity

A plea went out to the readers of the *East Budleigh and Budleigh Salterton Parish Magazine* in June 1898 after the death of William Till, of Knowle. He had died whilst in the prime of life, leaving a widow and nine children of whom only three were capable of earning a living; the eldest child was 12 years of age, the youngest an infant in arms. His widow was left with the task of raising six little children without a breadwinner in the family. Whilst the Board of Guardians had granted an allowance of 7s. a week, it would not be sufficient for the upbringing of the family as 'if the father had lived'. The vicar thought that the sum of £40, in addition to the Union allowance, would be enough to keep the family for three years so he therefore requested parishioners to donate whatever they could. Having already been promised 15 guineas, the vicar was counting 'on the charitable hearts and the sympathy of the Salterton people' to provide the outstanding £24.

The following month, however, the vicar reported that he had only received one subscription for the poor Mrs Till.

American Airmen

In September 1927 a monoplane, the *Pride of Detroit*, flown by William Brock and Edward Schlee, took off from Harbour Grace, Newfoundland, for England. This was the first stage of their flight around the world. The *Pride of Detroit* appeared over Budleigh Salterton on a Sunday at 7.30a.m. The aeroplane circled overhead, causing 'a considerable thrill' to the townsfolk. The pilots then dropped an orange from the plane. It was picked up by a boy who found a message inside it, in which the pilots enquired as to their whereabouts and requested directions to Croydon!

On-duty Coastguards used pebbles on the beach to give the airmen the requisite directions, and reinforced their message by chalking 'Budleigh Salterton' on the pavement. Having gathered the information by flying low, the pilots then headed across country towards Honiton.

Upon their arrival at Croydon, the airmen told of how they had lost their way and the events that had taken place at Budleigh Salterton. They had seen somebody chalk letters on the pavement and, for some reason, had read 'Seaton, Devon'.

A Pageant

In 1814 Budleigh Salterton held a pageant to celebrate the end of the Napoleonic Wars. Prior to this, Lord Rolle had intimated that he intended to give

1984 Gala Week: Noddy and Bigears. Left to right: *Margaret Atkins, Paul Meredith, Wendy Sampson, Betty Downing, Claire Hooking, Liz Edwards.*

(JULIA MEREDITH)

1987 Gala Week. Pictured are: *Kenneth Mcleod (TV personality) and Haley Lemon (Lions Gala Week Queen).*

(JULIA MEREDITH)

the village a treat, but owing to his absence, this did not take place for some time. Neighbouring towns on the coast had already held their celebrations, and cottagers loyal to king and country did not wish to delay. It was thought by the wealthier inhabitants of Budleigh Salterton, however, that it might have been better to postpone the festivity until the proclamation of peace. The cottagers though, having collected a subscription of about £30, carried out the arrangements for the ceremony themselves.

The Western Luminary, dated 4 June 1814, reported that Budleigh Salterton 'succeeded in displaying one of the most simple, natural, and therefore tasteful rural pageants that has yet been witnessed'. The procession was arranged with the

1994 Gala Week: Egyptian Extravaganza. Left to right, standing: *Agnes Gooding, Jeff Stacey, Dorothy Partridge, Betty Harrison, Nicola Callendar, Fiona Callendar, Gary Bond;* sitting: *Carol Snell, Julia Meredith, Cecily Pantol.*
(JULIA MEREDITH)

1998 Gala Week: Lights! Camera! Action! Left to right: *Shirley Snell, Julia Callendar, Dorothy Partridge, Carol Snell, Nigel Lemon, Julia Meredith, John Shiel, Angie Shiel, Lee Shiel, Tracy Shiel.*
(JULIA MEREDITH)

2002 Gala Week: Coronation Day. Left to right, coach: *Jordan Trick, Charlotte Meredith, Betty Harrison, Beverly Meredith;* standing: *Georgie Trick, Julia Meredith, Victoria Meredith, Hannah Barwick?, Shirley Snell, Nigel Lemon, Lisa Hooper, Nick Loman.* (JULIA MEREDITH)

2003 Gala Week: It's a Kind of Magic. Left to right, standing: *Lisa Hooper, Bethany Bolt, Victoria Meredith, Jake Shiel, Max Cooke, Lee Shiel* (with top hat); sitting: *Charlotte Meredith, Jordan Trick.* (JULIA MEREDITH)

greatest propriety and order, and consisted of:

The old postmaster, and an infirm tradesman, both on horseback – A boat... bearing the Union jack, and manned by a grey headed mariner at the stern, with four boys bearing blue oars – Sailors two and two – A car decked with laurel and laburnum, conveying old men and woman drawn by a horse led by two pages with the motto, 'The respect due to old age' – A soldier and sailor properly habited – Husbandmen with a plough and other implements of husbandry – Two farmers – Bassoons, french horns, clarionets, and other music – Builders, carpenters, and sawyers, with cross cut saw, etc., painters and glasiers – Tailors and shoemakers – Boys and Girls bearing placards inscribed 'Peace, love, and unity, faith, hope, and charity' – A shepherd and shepherdess – Young women two and two – Lacemakers – Little girls – Two footmen in handsome liveries bearing branches of flowering shrubs.

On parading through the village to Knowle and Budleigh, the procession returned through a triumphal arch of foliage and flowers to the lawn leading to Lord Rolle's chapel where 500 persons had

taken their places. The Revd Prebendary Dennis had been requested to attend and say grace.

The ceremony was followed by a picnic under an awning made from boat sails, after which a band played 'God Save The King'. 'Rule Britannia' and other popular airs were also played. At the end of the festivities the villagers left as they had arrived, in procession, and then:

paraded along the delightful walk on the beach, and let their neighbours, who crowded to see this village fete, perceive that they were not disqualified for walking in a straight line, they returned through the village to the lawn, where all dispersed, pleased with their entertainment and thankful for the public blessing from which it had arisen.

Thus a perfect day was ended.

Regattas

In Trewman's *Exeter Flying Post* of August 1850 it was reported of Budleigh Salterton that 'this interesting marine village presented an appearance of unusual

Budleigh Salterton before a storm, 1900s.
(STEVE RICHARDSON)

High waves at Budleigh Salterton, 1900s.
(STEVE RICHARDSON)

The beach after a gale, Budleigh Salterton, 1900s.
(STEVE RICHARDSON)

Methodist church choir bazaar, 1951. Left to right, back row: *Phyllis Trick, Alice Watts, Mary Trick, Amy Trick, Maurice Trick, Sally Pope, Mrs Hopkins, Mrs Hart, Mrs Jewell, Charlie Jewell, Cynthia Trick, ?, Harold Stapleton, ?, Mr Hopkins, Mr Keslake, Ken Trick;* middle row: *Ann Jewell, Shirly Dean, Mrs Stapleton;* front row: *Revd Smith, Edith Harris, Dick Leaman, Peter Hitt, Tom Bothwell, Mrs Standen, Miss Beamish, Violet Hitt, Winnie Leaman, Vera Pitman.*

(METHODIST CHURCH ARCHIVE)

animation from the many decorations, which had been called forth on the occasion of the Regatta'. No fewer than six arches were erected, adorned with numerous flags and surmounted by crowns of flowers. At the Rolle Arms a double arch had been constructed, whilst suspended from the arch on the promenade was a model of a vessel. Flags were profusely displayed upon the arches and across the streets from many windows.

Several yachts were in the harbour including *Fawn, Fluer de Marie, New Cut, Surprise* and *Swan*. The 'dead calm' which prevailed had hindered the arrival of other yachts that were to compete for the

'cup and purse of sovereigns', so the committee postponed the sailing matches. The rowing matches with four- and two-oared boats proceeded, as did the rural sports, to the great delectation of the hundreds of visitors who had thronged to the town.

To compensate for the lack of sailing, one band played on the sea, and the other at the top of the Rolle Arms Green, for those who were fond of dancing. A display of fireworks, manufactured and superintended by Mr Pulman of Exeter, a very clever pyrotechnist, gave great satisfaction to the crowd. The highlight of the display was a beautifully coloured crown underneath which was a ship, firing

Methodist church choir, 1958. Left to right, back row: *Maurice Trick, Ken Trick, Albert Hitt, Frank Keslake, Geoff Carter, Dick Leaman, Charlie Jewell, Denis Hopkins, Harold Stapleton, Chris Bolt, Tom Bothwell;* middle row: *Bertram Mears, Brian Hopkins, Mary Trick, Phyllis Trick, Alice Watts, Lucy Jewell, Ann Jewell, Val Watts, Christine Watts, Win Leaman, Phyliss Hope, Gillian Bothwell, Alan Tilbury, David Trick;* front row: *Vera Pitman, Florence Colley, Mrs Stapleton, Violet Hitt, Revd Smith, Mrs Smith, Frances Jewell, Edith Harris, Amy Trick, Jennifer Hitt, Janet Miller, Margaret Watts.*
(METHODIST CHURCH ARCHIVE)

Harvest Festival, 1981. Left to right, back row: *Harry Trick, Ken Trick, Mary Trick, Dick Leaman, Maurice Trick;* front row: *Winnie Trick, Phyllis Trick, Kath Trick, Win Leaman, Ruby Drew.* At this time the Trick family were prevalent in The Temple choir and in this year they took part in the BBC2 series 'Family Band', a programme about families who were united through music.
(METHODIST CHURCH ARCHIVE)

Harvest Festival, 1956. Left to right: *Gladys Hitt, Tommy Bothwell, Nellie Jewell, Phyllis Trick, Dorothy Smith, Mrs Hawkes, ?, Revd Smith, Ethel Madge.*
(METHODIST CHURCH ARCHIVE)

Methodist Youth Club birthday party, 1950s. Left to right, back row: *Len Haysom, Theo Lawrence, ? Cooksley, Adrian Haysom, Robert Bond, Ethel Bond, Alan Tilbury, ?, ?, ?;* fourth row: *Jenny Hitt, ?, David Trick, Margaret Watts, Valerie Watts, Alice Watts, Eddie Watts;* third row: *Brian Hopkins, Margaret Down, Norman Bolt, Janet Miller, Christine Watts, Maureen Haysom, Dorothy Smith, Revd Smith, Mrs Salter, ?;* second row: *Jeff Salter, Gillian Bothwell, Rosemary Pearcey, ?, ?, Marian Collins:* front row: *Sue Bond, Sylvia Oakes, David Veale, Bertram Mears, Rosemary Tayor, ?.* (METHODIST CHURCH ARCHIVE)

Methodist Youth Club birthday party, 1960s. Seated, clockwise from end of table: *Adrian Haysom, Tony Gooding, Margaret Down, Jeff Salter, Gillian Bothwell, ?, Jenny Hitt, ?, ?, ?, Val Priddis, Chris Dolling, Peter Dolling, ?, Margaret Waits, Bertram Mears.* (METHODIST CHURCH ARCHIVE)

Women's Institute, 1966. Left to right, back row: *Vera Vinnicombe, Kath Gooding, Miss Greenwood, Ivy Brown, Ida Bailey, Hilda West, Jo Freeman, Mattie Smith, Kitty Saunders, Lily Rogers, Heather Horne, Olive Skudder, Jean Lunnon;* middle row: *Vera Pitts, Kathleen Deller, Mrs Graham?, ?, ?, ?, ?, Doris Cowd, Mrs White, ?, Mrs Baker, Daisy Carnell, ?, Beryl Carpenter, Vera Curtis, ?, Madeline Godfrey;* front row: *Sue Fahey, Mrs Gooding, Edith Veale, Doris Hallet, Doris Fahey, Gladys Lunnon, Win Alford, Joan Ivings, Joyce Ivings, Jean Sage, Wendy Freeman, Marjorie Fowles, Lillian Hooker.* (KATH GOODING)

Women's Fellowship, 1995. Left to right, back row: *Clarice Hawkes, Mrs Baker, Hazel Duffin, Dot Sadd;* third row: *Win Leaman, Margaret Challoner, Irene Capstack, Anita Challoner, Kath Trick, Gladys Hitt, Mrs Prescott, Min Burgess;* second row: *Edith Rowe, Mrs O'Leary, Ruby Drew, Mrs Wilkinson, Mrs Davey, Jo Harvey-Williams, May Archer, Esme Burridge;* front row: *Ethel Madge, Mrs Jones, Mrs Jones, Mrs Piggot, Mrs Prior, Ethel Bond, Hilda Doughty.* (METHODIST CHURCH ARCHIVE)

from her portholes, and the word 'Farewell'.

The cup was sailed for on the following Friday. In addition to the yachts listed above, the *Blue Belle* and *Mt. Roebuck* also took part. The *Fawn* was declared the winner of the contest by three minutes.

Two years' later the regatta was again postponed 'on account of the unfavourable state of the weather'. When it did eventually take place, Mr Bell's *Secret* won the silver cup for first-class yachts, after beating the *Heroine* which had his father on board. The second class was won by Mr Shears's *Lily of the Valley*. Mr Middleton's *Fair Maid* took first place among the first-class punts, and Mr Algon's *Salterton* took first in the second-class race. The first prize for four-oared mackerel boats was won by G. Bence's *Teaser* and the four-oared gigs by Mr Ratcliff's *Victory*. The proceedings concluded with a dance where a large party assembled and remained until dusk.

The Golf Links, 1900s.   (Steve Richardson)

Another view of the Golf Links, late 1920s.

(Steve Richardson)

Shipwrecks

The wreck of the *Independiente*, driven ashore off Budleigh Salterton during gales was sold by auction for about £280 in January 1856.

Another wreck, the brigantine *Kingston* of Cardiff, with her masts, sails, rigging, anchors, chains etc. was put up in lots to be sold by auction on the beach at Budleigh Salterton during July 1862 'for the benefit of whom it may concern'.

A Royal Visit

The Prince of Wales inspected ex-service men at Budleigh Salterton during his visit on 16 and 17 May 1921. The Prince of Wales expressed his sympathy to Mr J. Marker who had been an invalid for four years 'owing to hardships undergone during the fighting on the Somme'.

On the first day of his visit the Prince played a 13-hole game of golf at the East Devon Golf Links with Sir Lionel Halsey as his opponent. On the following evening the full 18-hole course was played by the Prince accompanied by the club secretary, Major Gay, against Sir Lionel accompanied by Mr Persey, the club pro. The secretary received a signed photo of the prince whilst a tie pin with the royal cypher was given to the club pro.

Sunday School

Budleigh Salterton's Sunday school included a library and shoe club, as did Knowle Sunday school. (In 1898 the shoe club had 40 members who were doubtless of the poorer classes. It is possible that by clubbing together they were able to purchase shoes cheaper by buying in bulk.) During August 1888 the Budleigh Salterton Sunday school's annual treat was an outing to Otterton Park. The girls were taken to the park in brakes, thanks to a lady member of the congregation, and the boys went in wagons. An excellent tea and a variety of sports and games made the treat a great success.

The Youth's Recreation Association

The Youth's Recreation Association was formed during the autumn of 1895 to offer 'wholesome recreation' to the youth of Budleigh Salterton during winter evenings. Lord Rolle had permitted the association to use part of the old Rolle Chapel, which had previously been enclosed for the use of the Band of Hope. The room was then kitted out as follows:

games and illustrated newspapers and magazines were supplied by various friends and well-wishers, notably an excellent bagatelle board lent by Mrs Gray. A horizontal bar and parallel bars were fixed by Mr Bennett.

There were two recreational sessions: boys between the ages of 13 and 17, were able to attend on two nights of the week; young men over 18 were allowed to attend just one evening a week. Weekly attendance at the junior level usually consisted of 30–40 members, whereas the senior sessions usually attracted about 12 boys. The classes were perhaps surprisingly superintended almost wholly by women, with only two men Mr Trick and Mr Ware, who organised the members in athletics and drill.

On 22 April 1896, the association's first 'break-up evening' took place. The members demonstrated drill, gymnastics and boxing, as well as music from a piano lent by Mrs Semple. A recitation by H. Griffin on 'Boys' Rights' caused much amusement in the audience, as did the local references in some of the concluding lines:

But come to Budleigh Salterton,
And here, good friends, you'll find
The boys have all the best of it,
The girls are left behind!
The boys have drill and single stick,
And bars and bagatelle,
And, thanks to Chief-boatman Trick,
We learn to use them well.
The ladies sometimes 'chuck us out,'
But only when it's fair,
And though we 'try it on' with them,
We always end up square.
For what they make us mind you see,
Is hands and faces clean,
Good temper and a civil tongue,
No conduct rude or mean.
And all are welcome, 'Prentice, Clerk,
Errand Boy, Fisher, Groom,–
So here's success to all who meet
In Salterton Old Church Room!

References:
Devon and Cornwall Notes and Queries (1910), vol.6, part 1.
East Budleigh and Budleigh Salterton Parish Magazine (issues dating from the period 1874–1892).
J. Richardson, *The Local Historian's Encyclopedia* (New Barnet, Historical Publications, 1986).
Volo Non Valeo, *We Donkeys in Devon* (Exeter & London, 1886).
Trewman's *Exeter Flying Post.*
Westcountry Studies Library: newspaper cuttings.

Boys' Brigade twins Nick and Bob Loman, c.1955.
(NICK LOMAN COLLECTION)

Kay Loman (centre*) handing over the 1st Budleigh Salterton Brownie pack to the new Brown Owl, Rosemary Hutchings-Webber* (sitting to her right), *with unit helper Sue Saunders* (to the left), *1992.*
(NICK LOMAN COLLECTION)

Subscribers

Zoe C. Aitken, Budleigh Salterton

Joan and Alf Ashbee, Budleigh Salterton, Devon

Miss Ada, Terry and Ann Bastin

Francis and Mary Bennion, Budleigh Salterton

Bethany M. Bolt, Budleigh Salterton, Devon

Patrick N. Boone, Budleigh Salterton

Dee Bowker, Budleigh Salterton, Devon

A.W.N. Branson, 'Windrush', Budleigh Salterton

Sonia R. Brookes, Budleigh Salterton

Ron Browring, Budleigh Salterton

K.J. Burrow, Bucks Cross, Devon

Ronald (Nick) Carter, Budleigh Salterton

Rev. Robert S.J. Charles

Mr J. Collins, Cholsey, Oxfordshire

The Collins Family, Budleigh Salterton

Mrs Elsie Corfield, Budleigh Salterton, Devon

W.K.H. Coxe

Kevin Curran, Budleigh Salterton, Devon

Alan C. Davie, Budleigh Salterton, Devon

Mr and Mrs S.B. Davies, Budleigh Salterton, Devon

Alice Cosford Gittoes Davies, Budleigh Salterton

Stuart and Janet Day, Sidmouth

Valerie Dicks, Budleigh Salterton

John and Kay Douglas, Budleigh Salterton, Devon

Reginald Edds, Budleigh Salterton, Devon

C.M. Emuss, Knowle, Budleigh Salterton

Marilyn England, Budleigh Salterton, Devon

Doreen Evans, Budleigh Salterton, Devon

Mr Stephen J. Folland, Budleigh Salterton

Dr Simon Franklin, Budleigh Salterton, Devon

Peter and Susan Freeman, Knowle Village, Budleigh Salterton

Christina Garrod, Budleigh Salterton, Devon

John William Gatter, Budleigh Salterton

Doris K. Godfrey, Budleigh Salterton

Ken Gooding, Chalfont St Peter, Buckinghamshire

B.M. Hawkes

Richard O.G. Hayter

Margaret and Matthew Heaton, Budleigh Salterton

Roger Hodge, Dunsford

Priscilla Hull (née Carter), Budleigh Salterton

Mrs D.G. Imray

Mr and Mrs John H. Jewell, Teignmouth, Devon

Councillor Alan Jones, Town Mayor 2004

Emily L. Jones, Ting Tong, Budleigh Salterton

The Jones Family, Western Australia

Kathleen Laver, Budleigh Salterton

Winifred A. Leaman, Budleigh Salterton

Rosalyn Ann Lomas, Budleigh Salterton

P.H. Ludlow, Budleigh Salterton, Devon

Barbara A. Madell, Budleigh Salterton, Devon

P.S. McMillan, Exmouth, Devon

Denis M. Mears

Paul M. Meredith, Budleigh Salterton, Devon

Mrs P. Moore, Budleigh Salterton

Geoff and Denise Morris, Exmouth

Mrs Diana M. Moxon

Peter and Pearl Norman, Budleigh Salterton

Tom and Monica Oakes, Budleigh Salterton

Thomas F. Pearman, Budleigh Salterton

Victor C. Pegna, Budleigh Salterton, Devon

Michael and Brenda Peskin, Westbourne Terrace, Budleigh Salterton

William P. Prew, Budleigh Salterton

Wendy M. Pring, Budleigh Salterton
Kenneth Procter, Budleigh Salterton, Devon
Mrs Lynda Read and Mrs Phyliss Baker
Diana Richards, Budleigh Salterton
Ian Richards, Budleigh Salterton, Devon
Mr Arthur King Robinson, The Old Clink, Budleigh Salterton, Devon
D.M. Salter, East Budleigh
Margery Sawyer, Exmouth
Brigitte H. Schramke, Budleigh Salterton
Graham Searle, Budleigh Salterton, Devon
John W.N. Sedgemore, Exmouth, Devon
Mr Percy Sedgemore, Budleigh Salterton
Rosemary Smith
Ronald John Smith, Kersbrook, Budleigh Salterton
Shirley and John Snell, Budleigh Salterton
Joyce Stanley, Budleigh Salterton, Devon
Judith Stewart-Young
Rodney and Sonia Stone, Budleigh Salterton
Conrad and Julia Thomas, Budleigh Salterton
Arthur H.J. Vickers, Budleigh Salterton, Devon
Joan Walker
Richard Waller
John F.W. Walling, Newton Abbot, Devon
David Watson
Mr and Mrs Arthur Watts, Budleigh Salterton, Devon
Mrs Hazel M. Weeks
Bill West, Budleigh Salterton

In order to include as many historical photographs as possible in this volume, a printed index is not included. However, the Devon titles in the Community History Series are indexed by Genuki.

For further information and indexes to various volumes in the series, please visit: http://www.cs.ncl.ac.uk/genuki/DEV/indexingproject.html

The answer to the riddle on p.143 is 'Otter'.